THE MESSERSCHMITT Bf 110
IN COLOR PROFILE · 1939-1945

THE MESSERSCHMITT BF 110
IN COLOR PROFILE · 1939-1945

John Vasco & Fernando Estanislau

Schiffer Military History
Atglen, PA

Book design by Robert Biondi.

Library of Congress Catalog Number: 2005928605.

Printed in China.
ISBN: 0-7643-2254-0

We are always looking for people to write books on new and related subjects. If you have an idea for a book, please contact us at the address below.

Published by Schiffer Publishing Ltd.
4880 Lower Valley Road
Atglen, PA 19310
Phone: (610) 593-1777
FAX: (610) 593-2002
E-mail: Info@schifferbooks.com.
Visit our web site at: www.schifferbooks.com
Please write for a free catalog.
This book may be purchased from the publisher.
Please include $3.95 postage.
Try your bookstore first.

In Europe, Schiffer books are distributed by:
Bushwood Books
6 Marksbury Ave.
Kew Gardens
Surrey TW9 4JF
England
Phone: 44 (0)20 8392-8585
FAX: 44 (0)20 8392-9876
E-mail: Bushwd@aol.com.
Free postage in the UK. Europe: air mail at cost.
Try your bookstore first.

Foreword

by Martin Drewes

With a wry smile I still like to remember the day when I was able to achieve my oldest, dearest dream to become a pilot.

After my promotion to Second-lieutenant in a Panzer regiment, I obtained my transfer to the Luftwaffe on 1st September 1939, just as the war began.

Thoroughly prepared through many training hours, we learned how to fly most of the different types of aircraft of all sizes. One day, I had my first meeting with the Messerschmitt 110, the combat aircraft that I would fly on all my missions until the end of the war.

The Messerschmitt 110 soon became a multi-purpose aircraft, being used as a heavy fighter, bomber escort, ground-attack aircraft and it also served in a reconnaissance role. The experience of the 'Battle of Britain', and the necessity to build up a night defence against bomber attacks led the Bf 110 to its ultimate role: night fighter.

According to the circumstances, equipment was changed, often leading to improvements. There was no comparison between the Bf 110 that I flew at the end of 1940 during my training in the '*Zerstörerschule*' and my last Bf 110G-4 that I flew in combat in April 1945 – what a difference!

We were allowed to 'prepare' our Bf 110 according to our experiences on night missions. So, I had my aircraft polished and had the heavy armour plates taken out in order to increase speed. The two 30mm cannon were replaced with two 20mm cannon, and two 20mm '*Schräge Musik*' cannon, firing vertically, were fitted.

I remember with fondness my old 'friend', the Messerschmitt 110, and quite a few of the momentous events we had together that I survived. This meticulous work shows the interesting development of the Messerschmitt 110.

Martin Drewes

Introduction

John Vasco

When I was asked by Schiffer to undertake a 'Profiles' book on the Messerschmitt 110, I accepted the commission, on the basis that I would only proceed with it once a commercial artist of sufficient ability was found to produce the profiles. Through Sergio Luis Dos Santos, a dedicated Luftwaffe researcher, I was introduced to Fernando Estanislau. Upon seeing an example of his work, I had no doubt that he was the person to work with to bring this project to fruition. The reader will see within these pages the reasons I was excited to work with Fernando. His attention to detail is incredible, and he displays a genuine talent for this kind of work. I feel certain that this work is only the start of an illustrious career in this field, and Schiffer is indeed fortunate to be able to call on the abilities of Fernando, and Claes Sundin, in providing profiles for their work.

The Messerschmitt 110 has always appeared to be an enigma in the armoury of the Luftwaffe. At various times in its history it vacillated between being the hunter and the hunted. In the early months of the war it fulfilled all that was asked of it, albeit even then at the cost of many losses. Its young crews entered the Battle of Britain with a certain amount of optimism, but found the RAF fighters more than a match at taking them on in combat, and *Zerstörer* units suffered heavily. However, out of that there emerged a concept at which the Bf 110 proved very adept: that of the fighter-bomber, as evidenced by the relatively successful unit, *Erprobungsgruppe* 210. At the same time, the nascent night fighter force was progressing, and in this role the aircraft would prove to be ideally suited to the 'stealth in the night' role required to hunt down enemy bombers. Success in the ground attack role on the Russian front by the '*Wespengeschwader*' could not turn the tide on that front in the later war years. The operations in the Mediterranean area proved that despite the bravery of the crews employed there, the ultimate dominance of the Allied air forces in that theatre proved decisive. The final bloodletting of the daytime Bf 110 crews occurred in Defence of the Reich duties, as heavy losses were suffered when intercepted by the RAF and USAAF escorting fighters. The only hope of success was to get to the bombers, and return to base without interception. The 1944 Bf 110 loss tables tell a sorry tale. The final episode in the aircraft's history was the 'Hunter' Bf 110 night fighter becoming the 'Hunted', with the introduction of the Mosquito night fighter into the bomber streams of the RAF.

Camouflage and Markings

The camouflage and markings of Luftwaffe aircraft has been the subject of discussion and debates for decades. It is perhaps very dangerous territory to go into. However to not examine such areas would mean the overall subject would remain incomplete.

In an area of research where comparatively little remains extant, it is difficult to be prescriptive on the whole range of issues connected to camouflage colours. It is worth stating here, therefore, that the camouflage colours shown in this work are the views of the authors alone: the reader may disagree with those views. Such is the nature of interpretation of black and white photographs of the time, coupled with what is known of the official colours that were used on aircraft. The difficulty in all of this, of course, is that it is not known what went on at unit level. Whereas researchers can attempt to be specific, groundcrew cared nothing for such matters. Who knows how often paint stocks were mixed when a batch of aircraft needed painting and there was insufficient stock of the required colours on hand. Were greens topped up with other greens? Were blue undersurfaces topped up with shades of white or grey? Such variables no doubt came into play, but to be able to distinguish such nuances is almost impossible. What is therefore presented is our views on the camouflage and markings on a range of Messerschmitt 110 aircraft, which not only shows the evolving camouflage, but also the many variations in the types, indeed within the types, flown.

The profiles are heavily slanted towards the first years of the war, since that was the time of the greatest number of '*Zerstörer*' units. From the Battle of Britain onwards there was a gradual reduction in the number of daytime Bf 110 units. Another consideration in presenting the profiles was the availability of photographs that were able to show all of the necessary details to produce a profile. Many photographs presented excellent 'part views' of aircraft, but had to be dismissed from the project for lack of complete information.

Acknowledgements
The following are respectfully thanked for their contributions to this work: Peter Cornwell, George Hopp, Jim Kitchens, Ron Mackay, Ken Merrick, and Sergio Luis dos Santos. Recognition is also due to Heinz Mankau and Peter Petrick for their excellent reference work, *Messerschmitt Bf 110/Me 210/Me 410* which has helped to clarify details of the many sub-variants of the Bf 110.

• • •

Fernando Estanislau

When John Vasco asked me if I wanted to illustrate a book about the Bf 110, I couldn't imagine the huge task that would soon be in my hands. Two and a half years after that, I was finally writing these words having finished more than one hundred line drawings, researched and discovered many things about the *Zerstörer*, and collected much more doubts that remained – and maybe will remain forever – without answer.

About half of this period was spent creating the files that would generate the profiles. I soon realized that most of the available sources had discrepancies with the drawings on them, many mistakes and principally misinterpretation if compared directly to pictures. I decided to draw an entirely new set of side views that would cover everything from B to G aircraft – including sub-variants – using photography as a primary source instead of previous published drawings.

A difficult and repetitive task during the entire job was to scrutinize hundreds of pictures, compare them with the historical and technical data and finally settle on which interpretation was the most appropriate for each aircraft. Many times I had to override my personal interpretation and accept the historical document that provided different information. On the other hand, on more than one occasion a document guided my perception and made me see a detail that would otherwise have been overlooked.

The rest of the time was spent drawing codes, emblems and many small variations of crosses and letters, giving them colour and finally bringing the profiles to life.

However, even taking great care over each detail, black and white pictures are much trickier than people can imagine. During the war there were different kinds of photographic films that were sensitive in different ways, and the use of coloured lens filters wasn't uncommon. Diverse light throughout the day resulted in diverse nuances for the same colour or, on the contrary, identical appearance for different colours. With different laboratories and different materials being used in the development process all the time, different exposures were bound to produce different results. Additionally, each photograph is more than fifty years old, so its own ageing must also be considered. There are much more situations that could possibly change the appearance of an image, but just these related above are enough to amplify the difficulty it represented.

So, the profiles in this book should be seen as inspiration, not the final word. In the following years more images will appear, documents will be found, and our eyes will change the way of looking at all those black and white images. This book is an attempt to bring some colour to one of the most momentous periods in the history of mankind. I hope to have succeeded in this task.

Bf 110 Colours and Markings Note

Generally speaking, the evolution of the camouflage colours in the Luftwaffe during World War II is not complicated. However, the regular lack of observance of the rigid standards resulted in so many variations that RLM colours and their application are an infinite field of discussion. In the case of the Bf 110, little variation is seen, especially if compared with other aircraft in the same period. However, if looked upon individually, a myriad of small variations make each aircraft unique.

The present work touches upon many of these questions, and the following words trace a general view of the colours applied to the Bf 110, and the decisions made during the creation process.

Early 'B' and 'C' aircraft are assumed to be camouflaged in RLM 70 and RLM 71, the two official colors for the period. However, it is very hard to distinguish the pattern of the dark greens in most of the photographs available. A specific factory-standard document for the Bf 110 in unknown. Since each profile was constructed from a balance of documentary data and what is seen in the picture, some aircraft on the following pages will appear to have more solid camouflage, and others will show more contrast between the two colours. I have tried to replicate this in order to reflect all that is evident in the photographs.

During a relatively short period at the beginning of the war, the *Balkenkreuz* changed its shape and the underwing cross progressively decreased in size. It is common to see them painted in gloss black paint, together with the code letters, in an evident contrast with the flat paint used for the RLM 70 and 71 colours. The pace of life at that time meant that aircraft in the same *Staffel* were seen flying with different kinds and positions of crosses. Even later on, in a more individual context, deviations from standard practise appeared, and I have attempted to reproduce them as they were seen.

Although not always visible in photography, the third coloured individual letter was usually repeated not only under but also on the upper surfaces of the wings, usually in black, but also seen in other colours. This practice was progressively abandoned, but would still appear on the odd occasion in the later years. Many exceptions were to be seen, such as aircraft of *Erprobungsgruppe* 210 using blue individual letters on the fuselage and white underwing codes. The same applies to the spinners, which carried the *Staffel* colours completely or only on the tip. For obvious reasons, sometimes it is not possible to guarantee absolutely that the pictured aircraft carried the spinner in a particular colour or had underwing codes. When that is the case, estimation was made based on other pictures of related aircraft.

During the production run of C aircraft, sometime in 1940, the dark upper camouflage began to be substituted for a lighter version using what is believed to be RLM 02 and RLM 71, the lower surfaces remaining in RLM 65. The general pattern of the camouflage would follow the same general rules up to the end of the War: a disruptive pattern over the wings and fuselage, and a mottle of the same colours together with RLM 02 going down each side of the aircraft.

In an effort to make the aircraft more identifiable to friendly aircraft during the battle, different markings would appear. For a relatively short period, square yellow areas were applied to the rudders (mainly seen on ZG 26 Bf 110s), and the nose was painted in white. Aircraft in the Mediterranean had their engine cowlings painted yellow and many times rudder, elevators and ailerons were also seen in a different colour to the standard camouflage.

Of aircraft operating in desert areas, the first batch remained in European camouflage, and it is believed that improvisation using local paints was made on Luftwaffe aircraft. Official colours were RLM 78, a somewhat darker blue, and RLM 79, a sand colour that was commonly applied over all the upper surfaces going lower and even covering the sides of the engines and fuselage. Apparently, the use of the third desert colour RLM 80 – a dark green, common for other Luftwaffe aircraft, didn't find the same acceptance in the Bf 110 camouflage.

During the middle of 1941, culminating in an official instruction in November, new colours for the camouflage started to appear. The lighter and greyish RLM 74 and 75 would replace the previous dark greenish colours. For the undersides, a lighter RLM 76 blue would replace the previous RLM 65. However, it is not uncommon to clearly see both camouflages on different aircraft together in the same photograph. This phase was, as had happened before, a transition. As a result, especially during this period, many times it was impossible to distinguish which of the two colour combinations the aircraft was painted in. When that happened, the final decision was made based on a mix of all information available (such as theatre of operation, period, version of the aircraft, analysis of other related images, etc.) and every effort was made to state the most likely camouflage.

In addition, during the research for this book, a not commonly related aspect became evident. Even wearing new 74/75/76 colours, many aircraft after 1942 received an application of a lighter colour, possibly the previously used RLM 02, or an even lighter shade, over its spine and wings. Far from being a local procedure or exception, examples were widespread and in different units.

The tactical markings would change from yellow bands for the Eastern front to white bands for the Mediterranean theatre, applied usually on the rear part of the fuselage. Again, local (or specific for an aircraft) variations were reported concerning its position and size. For example, aircraft of the ZG 1 in Russia had their yellow bands mainly placed just aft of the wing root, a procedure rarely seen in other units.

The under wing coloured tips, a common practice for other aircraft, appear to have been less commonly adopted, although there are some pictures with them clearly visible, for example JG 5 seems to have them on many aircraft, if not all. The best effort was made to detect if every aircraft had such markings. When its detection was impossible, even with modern software, the profile was made without it.

Also the under side of the engine cowlings were painted in yellow as an identification marking, a practice adopted with a certain degree of acceptance, especially in aircraft flying on the Eastern front.

These colours were mainly used for all Bf 110s until the end of the conflict, at least for day fighters. Night fighters however, adopted another set of colours. Beginning with the adoption of an entire black covering with grey code letters, the later aircraft in night fighter roles were painted in standard colour variations or RLM 76 overall with mottle, waves or a dot pattern in RLM 75, that sometimes was applied so thinned that it is hardly seen in the photograph. The first two fuselage codes, indicating the *Geschwader*, were reduced in size beginning sometime in 1943 – a rule that applied also to day fighters. Surprisingly, the light colour camouflage provided a much better protection in the dark sky than black paint.

In addition, some images demonstrate that, at least for a short period, there were night fighters with the underside of just one wing painted in black, probably to avoid misidentification.

Acknowledgments

I wish to thank everyone who was directly involved in my work. In particular, Goethe Eduardo Barroso, Othniel Costa, Leonardo de Oliveira Neves, Ataide Cirino Pereira and Helmut Karl Zierach for lending rare documentation to me for so long; Julio Junqueira for all our discussions concerning Luftwaffe history; Paulo Roberto Penna Coutinho Filho for his computer's hardware support and friendship; George Hopp for his reliable support and Martin Drewes for his sympathy and assistance with my queries.

In the Internet community, particularly in the forums, I wish to thank all who spent their time dealing with my questions, replying to my emails and helping in any way: Christoph Awender, Denilson Alberti, Jerry Crandall, Peter D.Evans, Jon Carr Farrelly, Ivan Ferrando, Ettore Giordano, Tomke Hahn, Jürgen, Willenm Kleijin, Rudolph Laursen, Leco, Robert Lundin, Randy Lutz, Eric Mombeek, Gustavo Morabito, Jerry Soetewey, Ricardo Trotta were all kind enough spending their time with me.

A special thanks to John Vasco, who had such tolerance with me and my questions – a quest for more and more details and pictorial proof for the details I reproduced.

Also all my gratitude goes to aviation researcher Sergio Luis dos Santos, truly a generous friend who arranged the first contact with John Vasco, shared his library and time providing dozens and dozens of books and pictures – I wouldn't have been able to do that much without his invaluable help.

Every single thing I have done in my illustrations is dedicated to my mother Telmar, who taught me life's first flying lessons, and whose own splendid flying I nowadays still try to imitate.

The Profiles

Type: B-1
Period: Winter 1939/40
Unit: Training unit, not known.
Crew: Not known.

This 'B' variant carries no armament in the nose. It also lacks a radio mast. The propeller blades appear to be either painted in primer only, or in bare metal. The swastika is in the early position of being placed across both fin and rudder. Note the oversize cross under the wing, which is placed further inboard than would later be the case. Note also the number '84' on the undersurface of the wing, outboard of the cross.

Type: B-1
Period: Not known.
Unit: Not known.
Crew: Not known.

Like the previous profile, this Bf 110 B carries no armament in the nose, and also lacks the *Bordfunker*'s machine gun. This training aircraft carries a number on the fuselage, as opposed to a letter as seen in the previous profile. The W.Nr., indecipherable, is seen above the swastika, which has been applied across both fin and rudder. The recess for the rearward firing machine gun can be seen immediately aft of the cockpit in this view.

Type: B-1
Period: Not known.
Unit: Not known.
Crew: Not known.

The camouflage pattern on this 'B' would tend to indicate a period of 1940 or later. This aircraft carries a *Stammkennzeichen* (four letter code, usually applied at the point of manufacture) on the fuselage and a white rear fuselage band, with the swastika on the fin only.

Type: B-1
Period: Early 1940.
Unit: 2. *Staffel, Zerstörerergänzungsgruppe*
Crew: *Unteroffizier* Paul Wenke (Pilot)
Obergefreiter Hans Heinrich (*Bordfunker*)

This B of *Zerstörerergänzungsgruppe* carries both a number and *Stammkennzeichen* on the fuselage. As in the previous views, this aircraft carries no armament, and lacks a radio antenna. The crew remained together at the end of their training, being posted to 4. *Staffel*, *Zerstörergeschwader* 76. Hans Heinrich survived the war; the fate of Paul Wenke is not known. Again, the camouflage pattern of this aircraft is difficult to discern.

Left: Head-on view of Paul Wenke at the controls of a Bf 110, with Hans Heinrich behind him.

Type: B-1
Period: Early 1940.
Unit: 5. *Staffel*, *Zerstörergeschwader* 26
Crew: *Oblt*. Eberhard von Treutschler d'Elsa (pilot) (*Staffelkapitän*)
Ofw. Hermann Roßler (*Bordfunker*)

A 'B' in service with an operational unit. Although the photograph is of indifferent quality, it tends to show that the upper surface camouflage was a single colour. Red, the standard 5. *Staffel* colour at the time, is carried as the individual aircraft letter, without any outline to it, and the 5. *Staffel* '*Pik-As*' emblem is carried on the nose. *Hptm*. D'Elsa was shot down on 18th May 1940 seriously wounded into French captivity, and although released some weeks later, he did not return to combat duties again due to the severity of his injuries.

Right: Hauptmann Eberhard von Treutschler d'Elsa seen during the Western campaign in early May 1940.

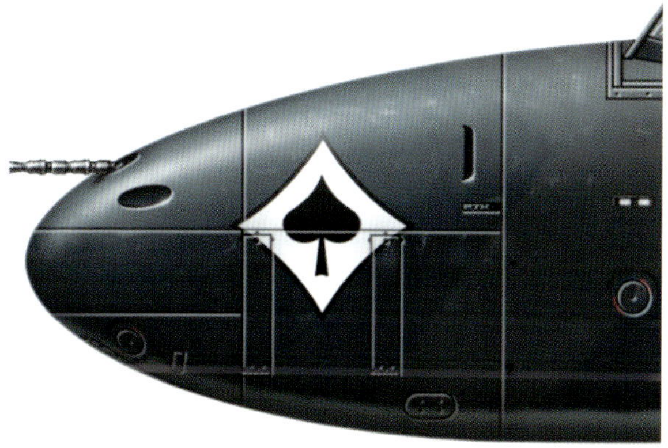

Type: B-1
Period: Early 1940.
Unit: *Stab*, II.*Gruppe*, *Zerstörergeschwader* 26
Crew: *Oberleutnant* Wilhelm Schaefer (Pilot)
Bordfunker not known

Another 'B' in the service of ZG 26. This is the aircraft of the *Gruppenadjutant*, Wilhelm Schaefer. In the *Gruppenstab* of II./ZG 26 in early 1940, the aircraft of the *Gruppenkommandeur*, Friedrich Vollbracht, 3U+AC, carried a single red lightning flash on its nose; Schaefer's 'B' carried one in yellow. When Vollbracht was posted to the *Kommodore*'s position in ZG 2, he took Schaefer with him as his *Geschwaderadjutant*, and they both continued the practise of having single lightning flashes on the nose of their aircraft in that unit. The individual aircraft letter 'B' is in the *Gruppenstab* colour of green, as are the propeller spinners. Note on this 'B' that the swastika is on the fin only. Note once again the apparent lack of a W.Nr. on either the fuselage or fin.

Right: Wilhelm Schaefer poses in front of his Bf 109 when with II./JG 142, showing the yellow lightning flash that he carried forward onto the Bf 110s that he flew as his personal aircraft throughout 1940.

Type: B-1
Period: Early 1940.
Unit: 3. *Staffel*, *Zerstörerergeschwader* 76
Crew: Not known.

In the photograph major work is taking place on the port engine of this Bf 110. Note the extreme positioning of the under-wing cross, and the individual aircraft letter inboard of it, a somewhat unusual occurrence. Also of interest is the thin white area of the fuselage cross, a feature of most Luftwaffe fighter aircraft at this time in the war. The *Staffel* colour of yellow is featured in the aircraft's individual letter on the fuselage and on the small ring on the propeller cover. Note also in the photograph the small wooden fin/rudder locks in place.

Type: C-1
Period: 1940.
Unit: 1. *Staffel*, *Zerstörerergeschwader* 76
Crew: Not known.

This C-1 carries the early style fuselage cross with narrower white areas. It can be identified as a 'C-1' variant due to the two antennae going to both the port and starboard fins. The insulation point on the port side can just be seen up and to the left of the letter 'M' of the fuselage code. Additionally, the small inlet on the rear of the port engine cowling is another feature of the 'C-1' variant only. The individual aircraft letter 'D' is solely white, with no outline. The photograph clearly shows two tone green (70/71) upper surface camouflage colours. The spinner tip is in the *Staffel* colour of white. The individual aircraft letter 'D' does not appear to be carried on the wing top surface.

Type: C-1
Period: 6th September 1939
Unit: 1. *Staffel*, *Zerstörergeschwader* 1
Crew: *Staffelkptn. Major* Karl Hammes (pilot)
Oberfeldwebel Walter Steffan (*Bordfunker*)

This belly-landed C-1, which was shot down on 6th September 1939, shows all the characteristics of an early Bf 110: solid camouflage down the sides of the fuselage; early style fuselage cross with small white surround to the black centre, and the swastika across both fin and rudder. The individual aircraft letter, 'I', is in the *Staffel* colour of white, as are the propeller caps; only the backplate is in black-green. In 1940 the propeller caps colour for this *Staffel* would change to white/blue/white. The photograph shows that groundcrew have already removed the armament. No W.Nr. can be seen on this aircraft.

Type: D-0
Period: Spring 1940.
Unit: 3. *Staffel*, *Zerstörerergeschwader* 76
Crew: Not known.

This '*Dackelbauch*' has the standard size fuselage cross of mid-1940 onwards, compared to that shown in the previous aircraft profile from the same *Staffel*. The *Staffel* colour of yellow is reflected in the individual aircraft colour, but not on the propeller. Note the distinctive 'ribbing' on the *Dackelbauch*. Note also that the black letters of the unit code have a distinctive sheen to them, appearing as almost a gloss finish.

Type: C-2
Period: May 1940
Unit: 6. *Staffel*, *Zerstörergeschwader* 26
Crew: Not known.

This aircraft carries all the markings that became standard in the Battle of Britain period on Bf 110s: swastika on the fin only; regulation sized fuselage cross; underwing cross not extending onto the flaps; W.Nr. on rear fuselage, and individual aircraft number and spinner tip in the *Staffel* colour. Note that the *Bordfunker*'s machine gun is 'parked' in the recess provided; in later variants that recess would be faired over. 3U+GN has the early port side aerial mast, indicating a 'C-1' version.

Type: C-2
Period: 13th May 1940.
Unit: 14. *Staffel*, *Lehrgeschwader* 1
Crew: *Unteroffizier* Hans Bechthold (Pilot)
Unteroffizier Wilhelm Harder (*Bordfunker*)

On 13th May 1940 *Unteroffizier* Bechthold overran the airfield on landing at Mannheim. Early style camouflage is carried with a full sized fuselage cross, and the swastika appears on the fin only. The crew survived this accident. Harder was killed in action on 21 July 1940; Bechthold parachuted into captivity over England on 27th September 1940. Note again that the black letters of the code appear to have a semi-gloss tint.

Type: C-1
Period: May/June 1940.
Unit: 1. *Staffel*, *Zerstörergeschwader* 1
Crew: Not known.

Photographed during the Western campaign, this aircraft carries the early war markings of the swastika across the fin and rudder and the earlier style fuselage cross with a smaller white area. Individual aircraft letter and spinner are in the *Staffel* colour of white, as is the girl's name on the nose of the machine. This aircraft was the regular machine for ground crew man Willi Falkenroth to service.

Type: C-1
Period: June 1940.
Unit: 15. *Staffel*, *Lehrgeschwader* 1
Crew: Not known.

This well-known view of L1+CL shows several interesting variations to standard practise of the time. The black centre to the fuselage cross is oversize, in contrast to the unit code, which appears to be thinner than usual. The fuselage camouflage would appear to have been originally a single overall colour all the way down the fuselage, which has been oversprayed with the undersurface colour RLM 65, then crudely overpainted with a brush. The engine cowling carries a solid top surface colour. The small *Gruppe* emblem, a wolf's head, can be seen on the forward fuselage. The yellow spinner and individual aircraft letter conform to the normal colour practise of the time. The revised port side aerial masts on the other aircraft indicate 'C-2' variants.

Type: C-1
Period: June 1940.
Unit: 5. *Staffel*, *Zerstörergeschwader* 1
Crew: *Feldwebel* Manfred Dähne (Pilot)
Obergefreiter Herbert Klinke (*Bordfunker*)

This aircraft was brought down over Swiss airspace on 8th June 1940 following the incursion of a mixed Luftwaffe force over that country. Dähne and Klinke had been in combat with Swiss Bf 109 Es, and had also been hit by Flak. Both were interned in Switzerland for a short time before being returned to Germany. Upon his return, Klinke lodged a claim for a Swiss Bf 109. Because of his injuries, Klinke did not return to active service for several months. In the meantime, Dähne continued to fly missions and was shot down and killed over England on 25th August 1940 with *Bordfunker Unteroffizier* Fritz Müller while flying with 8. *Staffel*, *Zerstörergeschwader* 76. Klinke later flew on the Russian front and on one occasion became seriously ill one night, resulting in his hospitalisation for a time. The next day his pilot took off on a mission with a different *Bordfunker* and they have been posted missing ever since. Klinke survived the war but always claimed he was a very lucky man indeed! Herbert Klinke died aged eighty-three in April 2002. This aircraft has two-tone green upper surfaces, and carried the first version of the '*Wespe*' emblem on the nose: three small wasps above clouds, designed by *Leutnant* Richard Marchfelder. The individual aircraft letter 'G' is black outlined with white, and the W.Nr. 2831 appears on the rear fuselage. The *Bordfunker*'s rear canopy is the fully enclosed version; there would be changes to it in later variants of the Bf 110.

Above: Dähne and Klinke with Swiss officials. Note Klinke's bandaged left hand and arm.

Type: C-1
Period: June 1940.
Unit: 1. *Staffel*, *Zerstörergeschwader* 1
Crew: Not known.

The cause for such a '*Fliegerdenkmal*' shown in the photograph was usually heavy braking on soft ground. Differences to the previous ZG 1 aircraft are the individual aircraft letter being in blue, outlined in white, and the propeller spinners being in the revised colours of white/blue/white. These markings would be carried forward when the *Staffel* formed the 1. *Staffel* of *Erprobungsgruppe* 210 in July 1940. This aircraft carries the early style fuselage cross and the swastika across both fin and rudder. A single white victory bar adorns the fin.

Type: C
Period: Summer 1940.
Unit: 8. *Staffel*, *Zerstörergeschwader* 76
Crew: Not known.

II. *Gruppe*, *Zerstörergeschwader* 1 was re-designated III. *Gruppe*, *Zerstörergeschwader* 76 on 6th July 1940. However, the *Gruppe* retained its II. *Gruppe Staffel* identification letters ('M', 'N' and 'P') rather than changing them to the correct letters of 'R', 'S' and 'T'. This aircraft therefore shows the carryover from 5./ZG 1 to 8./ZG 76. A full sized fuselage cross is carried, but the spacing between the individual characters of the fuselage code is greater than normal. The top surface camouflage appears to be RLM 71/02, which became more prevalent as the Battle of Britain progressed. The other photograph, although of a different machine, gives an excellent close up view of the 'three wasps above a cloud' emblem.

Type: C-1
Period: Western Campaign, Spring 1940
Unit: *Gruppenstab*, I.*Gruppe*, *Zerstörergeschwader* 1
Crew: Not known.

This aircraft of the *Gruppenstab* has an early style of fuselage cross, and has the individual aircraft letter in black. The single chevron denotes the aircraft of the *Gruppenadjutant*, who at that time was *Oberleutnant* Siegfried Wandam. Twin aerial antennae, the small air scoop on the rear of the engine cowling, and the lack of the remote control for the D/F loop antenna on the port cockpit canopy all identify this machine as a 'C-1' variant.

Type: C-4
Period: 11th July 1940
Unit: 9. *Staffel*, *Zerstörergeschwader* 76
Crew: *Oberleutnant* Gerhard Kadow (*Staffelkapitän*) (pilot)
Gefreiter Helmut Scholz (*Bordfunker*)

This aircraft flown by the *Staffelkapitän* of 9./ZG 76 was damaged in combat on 11th July 1940 while flying escort for Ju 87s over the south coast of England, and Gerhard Kadow belly-landed at Grange Heath, near Lulworth. Both Kadow and Scholz survived into captivity. This aircraft, although flying with III. *Gruppe*, carries a II. *Gruppe Staffel* letter, 'P'. The individual aircraft letter of 'E' is in the *Staffel* colour of yellow, as are the spinner tips. The original '*Wespe*' emblem was carried on the nose of the aircraft. Two victory bars can be seen on the fin.

Type: C-5
Period: 21st July 1940
Unit: 4(F)./*Aufklarungsgruppe* 14
Crew: *Oberleutnant* Friedrich-Karl Runde (pilot)
Feldwebel Willi Baden (*Bordfunker*)

This reconnaissance Bf 110 came down at Home Farm, Goodwood, on 21st July 1940 following combat with Red Section of 238 Squadron. The strong contrast between the upper surface camouflage colours of 71 and 02 can clearly be seen. It is also an early example of mottled camouflage used by the type. This aircraft was later repaired and test flown by the RAF.

Type: C
Period: 16th August 1940
Unit: 9. *Staffel*, *Zerstörergeschwader* 76
Crew: *Oberleutnant* Urban Schlaffer (*Staffelkapitän*) (pilot)
Obergefreiter Franz Obser (*Bordfunker*)

This aircraft was engaged by 602 Squadron Spitfires and Schlaffer put down at Lee Farm, Clapham, near Worthing after suffering combat damage. The lighter colour on the fuselage sides, becoming more prevalent on a lot of Bf 110s as the Battle of Britain progressed, is evident on this machine. The old 6. *Staffel*, *Zerstörergeschwader* 1, identifying letter of 'P' is retained as the fourth character in the fuselage code. This should have changed to 'T' upon re-designation to 9. *Staffel*, *Zerstörergeschwader* 76.

Type: C
Period: 1940.
Unit: *Gruppenstab*, III. *Gruppe*, *Zerstörergeschwader* 26
Crew: Not known.

This aircraft carries the swastika on the fin only, and has the full size fuselage cross. The sides of the fuselage are in Blue 65, with the top surfaces in 71/02. Note the high demarcation of the upper surface camouflage on the starboard engine cowling. Note also in the photograph that the *Bordfunker*'s rear canopy has a revised design, with an open area in the central rear panel.

Type: C-1
Period: Spring 1940.
Unit: 1. *Staffel*, *Zerstörergeschwader* 76
Crew: *Leutnant* Hans-Ulrich Kettling (Pilot)
Obergefreiter Fritz Volk (*Bordfunker*)

Kettling (left in the photo, with Volk) flew this aircraft in the early months of 1940. It carries the standard top surface camouflage of the period, and the early style fuselage cross and placement of the swastika. Kettling and Volk flew mainly aircraft 'C' in 1. *Staffel*, and were flying Bf 110 D, M8+CH, W.Nr. 3155, when they were shot down on 15th August 1940 on an escort mission over the east coast of England. Note in this photograph the completely enclosed rear *Bordfunker*'s canopy, a feature of C-1 aircraft.

Type: C
Period: Summer 1940.
Unit: 6. *Staffel*, *Zerstörergeschwader* 26
Crew: Not known.

This aircraft displays the early 70/71 upper surface camouflage with full size fuselage cross and swastika on the fin only. The unit emblem, one of the four suits in a pack of cards: a diamond but placed on its side, was carried on the forward fuselage. The individual aircraft letter 'G' has no outline to it. Note the early, fully enclosed rear canopy for the *Bordfunker* in the photograph.

Type: C-2
Period: Summer 1940.
Unit: 2. *Staffel*, *Zerstörergeschwader* 2
Crew: Not known.

Early style upper surface camouflage is carried on this Bf 110, W.Nr. 2134. Note that the *Bordfunker*'s central rear section of the canopy has been removed. It would appear that this was a modification made in the field by some units, and appeared to be particularly favoured by *Erprobungsgruppe* 210.

Type: C
Period: Summer 1940.
Unit: 6. *Staffel*, *Zerstörergeschwader* 76
Crew: Not known.

70/71 upper surface camouflage is carried by this 'Sharksmouth'. The individual aircraft letter and spinner tips are in the *Staffel* colour of yellow, with the letter 'D' having no outline to it. Note on this aircraft also the removal of the *Bordfunker*'s central rear section of the canopy.

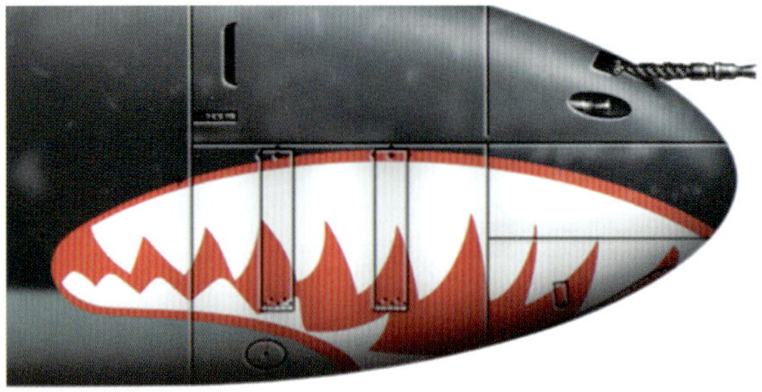

Type: C
Period: Summer 1940.
Unit: 6. *Staffel*, *Zerstörergeschwader* 76
Crew: Not known.

Yellow 'G' of 6. *Staffel* displays the same features as the previous profile, but carries an indistinguishable number of victory bars above the swastika.

Type: C
Period: Summer 1940
Unit: 14. *Staffel*, *Lehrgeschwader* 1
Crew: Not known.

The photograph at right clearly shows that the areas behind 'L1' and 'AK' have been oversprayed with the undersurface colour of 65 before the application of the unit code. The rest of the fuselage has a light covering of grey 02. The *Bord-funker*'s machine gun rests centrally, indicating that the revised central panel is in place, with the trough for the original storage place for the gun faired over. The fuselage cross appears to be a mix of the early style and standard 1940 style: it has neither the slim dimensions of the early style nor the full sized style that can be seen in later profiles.

Type: C-2
Period: Summer 1940.
Unit: *Gruppenstab*, V.*Gruppe*, *Lehrgeschwader* 1
Crew: *Hauptmann* Horst Liensberger (*Gruppenkommandeur*) (Pilot) *Unteroffizier* Albert Köpge (*Bordfunker*)

This aircraft shows the move to lighter fuselage sides, with a weak wash of an upper surface colour lightly brushed over the 65 sides. Forward of the cockpit this becomes almost non-existent. The *Gruppe* emblem of a small wolf's head remains on the nose of the aircraft. Note that the unit code characters are larger than the other two characters, a rather unusual situation. The individual aircraft letter of 'X' is in the *Gruppenstab* colour of green.

Type: C
Period: Spring 1940.
Unit: 2. *Staffel*, *Zerstörergeschwader* 52
Crew: Not known.

This 'C' displays the early style upper surface camouflage with full size fuselage cross and the swastika on the fin only. The distinctive dragon emblem of the unit is carried on the nose. I. *Gruppe* ZG 52 was redesignated II./ZG 2 at the beginning of the Battle of Britain and suffered heavy losses in the subsequent action over southern England.

Type: C
Period: Summer 1940.
Unit: 6. *Staffel*, *Zerstörergeschwader* 2
Crew: *Hauptmann* Eberhard Heinlein (*Staffelkapitän*) (pilot)
Bordfunker not known

ZG 2 flew a mix of 'C' and 'D' variants during the Battle of Britain. This aircraft was flown by the *Staffelkapitän* of 6. *Staffel*, *Hauptmann* Eberhard Heinlein. It carries a light mottle over the fuselage sides and a demarcation between the upper and lower surface camouflage routed around the swastika on the fin and rudder. Heinlein was killed when he crashed in this aircraft on a non-combat flight on 28th September 1940. Sitting in front of the aircraft is almost certainly the whole of 6. *Staffel* awaiting instructions.

Type: C-4
Period: Spring/Summer 1940.
Unit: 8. *Staffel*, *Zerstörergeschwader* 76
Crew: *Oberleutnant* Hans Münich (pilot)
Unteroffizier Adolf Käser (*Bordfunker*)

This aircraft carries the early style upper surface camouflage and full size fuselage cross. On 4th September 1940 Münich and Käser crash-landed in a Bf 110 , at Black Patch, near Angmering, with the same code, 2N+CN, but with a black 'C' outlined in white, and with the three wasps emblem on the nose, following combat over the south of England. It is not known whether that was the same aircraft as the one shown here, with updated markings. Münich and Käser both survived into captivity.

Type: C-4
Period: Summer 1940.
Unit: *Gruppenstab*, I. *Gruppe*, *Zerstörergeschwader* 2
Crew: *Oberleutnant* Gerhard Granz (*Gruppenadjutant*) (pilot)
Feldwebel Willi Schubel (*Bordfunker*)

Granz and Schubel baled out of this aircraft, W.Nr. 3246, on 7th September 1940, both surviving into captivity. It shows that the early style of camouflage was still being carried on Bf 110s into September 1940. The two-tone green can clearly be seen. Close examination of the central rear panel of the *Bordfunker*'s canopy shows that the metal frame does not extend fully around the panel, a development of the earlier style previously mentioned. Four white victory bars were carried on the port fin. In the photograph, Granz is on the left, with *Bordfunker* Schubel.

Type: D
Period: Summer 1940.
Unit: *Geschwaderstab, Zerstörer-geschwader* 26
Crew: Not known.

This aircraft has the revised 1940 camouflage with light mottle down the fuselage sides. It carries a single chevron, which usually denoted the aircraft of the Adjutant. The extended rear fuselage, common to the 'D' series, can be clearly seen in the photograph. Note also in the photograph the *Bordfunker* sitting facing forward, at the controls of the radios in the central section of the cockpit. Note also the strong contrast in the camouflage colours on the port wing, almost certainly 71/02.

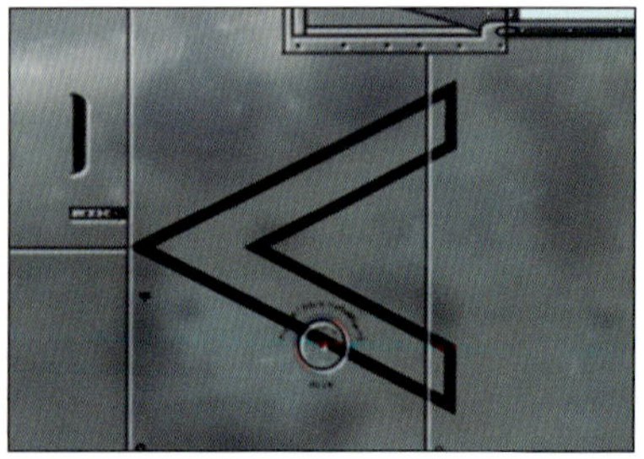

Type: D-0/B
Period: 21 July 1940, Battle of Britain.
Unit: 2. *Staffel*, *Erprobungsgruppe* 210
Crew: *Oberleutnant* Alfred Habisch (Pilot)
Unteroffizier Ernst Elfner (*Bordfunker*)

This aircraft was flown by Habisch and Elfner on missions in the early part of the Battle of Britain against shipping around the south and south-east coast of England. Upon return from one such mission on 21st July 1940, the aircraft suffered a collapsed starboard undercarriage after receiving hits from RAF fighters over the sea. The word 'Jaguar' on the nose, (which appears to be semi gloss, or gloss) was a humorous reference to the propaganda-inspired name for the fighter-bomber version of the Bf 110. Habisch and Elfner usually flew the 'C' of 2nd *Staffel*. The accompanying photograph shows clearly the bomb rack and red tips to the propeller spinners. Ernst Elfner is seen on the port wing root.

Left: Oberleutnant Alfred Habisch, pilot of S9+CK.

Type: D
Period: Summer 1940.
Unit: 2. *Staffel*, *Zerstörergeschwader* 76
Crew: Not known.

This aircraft displays the early style upper surface camouflage with later style features: full size fuselage cross and swastika on the fin only. The fuselage cross appears not to have any black outline to its white areas. The early 2. *Staffel* colour of red as the individual aircraft letter is carried, and spinner tip is also in red (black became the standard colour for 2. *Staffel* during 1940). The extended rear fuselage of the 'D' series can be seen on the photo.

Type: C-6
Period: 29 July 1940, Battle of Britain.
Unit: 1. *Staffel*, *Erprobungsgruppe* 210
Crew: *Leutnant* Erich Beudel (pilot)
Obergefreiter Heinrich Diemer (*Bordfunker*)

One of only 12 'C-6' variants built, carrying a single 30mm MG 101 cannon under the fuselage in place of the standard two 20mm cannon, this aircraft received damage in combat with Hurricanes of 151 Squadron off the south-east coast of England following an attack on a convoy on 29th July 1940. Beudel managed to crash-land at St. Omer-Arques. Diemer was wounded and spent time in hospital. He returned to duty with his former *Staffel*, then re-designated 1./ZG 1, and was posted missing in action on the Russian front on 19th September 1942 south of Kotluban. The C-6s with 1./ZG 1 were kept on charge with the *Staffel* when it was re-designated 1./Erpr. Gr. 210 on 1st July 1940, and the *Staffel* did not change the unit code on its aircraft from '2N' to 'S9' until early August 1940 when it took the first fighter-bomber variants on charge. Note the photograph shows clearly that the *Bordfunker*'s central rear canopy panel has been completely removed. This appeared to be a regular occurrence in the unit.

Far left: Leutnant Erich Beudel in the cockpit of a Bf 110. left: The only known photograph of Obergefreiter Heinrich Diemer.

Type: D
Period: Summer 1940.
Unit: 6. *Staffel*, *Zerstörergeschwader* 2
Crew: Not known.

This 'D' carries light coloured fuselage sides with a distinctive demarcation line between the upper and lower surface camouflage across the fin and rudder. The W.Nr. in white is carried on the rear fuselage. The individual aircraft letter 'B' carries no outline to it.

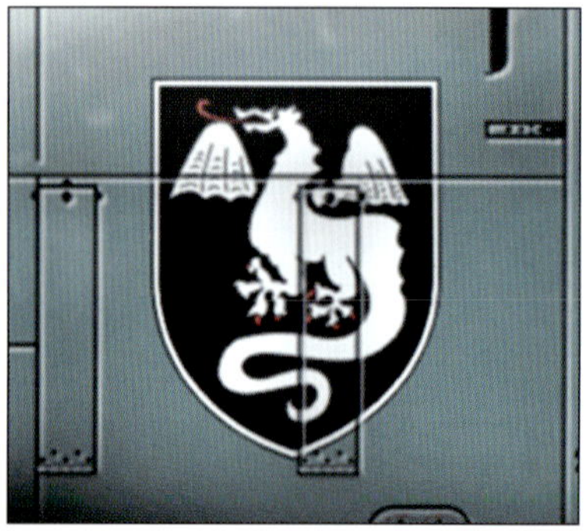

Type: C-6
Period: Battle of Britain.
Unit: 1. *Staffel*, *Erprobungsgruppe* 210
Crew: Not known.

Like the previous Bf 110 C-6 profile, this C-6 carries the early style upper surface camouflage and full size fuselage cross. Also shown are the white-blue-white propeller colours which were distinctive to this *Staffel*. The photograph also shows that this aircraft carried a gun-camera in the nose. The 30mm cannon found in the wreckage of the only 'C-6' to crash on mainland England (S9+TH following the raid on Croydon airfield on 15th August 1940) was positively identified by RAF Intelligence as, 'type MG 101 made by Rheinmetall Works'.

Type: D-0/B
Period: Battle of Britain.
Unit: *Gruppenstab*, *Erprobungsgruppe* 210
Crew: *Leutnant* Karl-Heinz Koch (pilot) (Technical Officer)
Unteroffizier Rolf Kahl (*Bordfunker*)

Left: The only known photograph of Leutnant Karl-Heinz Koch (centre of photo in peaked cap).

This aircraft, from the *Gruppenstab* of *Erprobungsgruppe* 210, was damaged in combat following the raid on Croydon in the early evening of 15th August 1940. Heading for France it was attacked once again by Flight Lieutenant Humphrey a'Becket Russell of the Biggin Hill Training Flight, and *Leutnant* Koch, Technical Officer of the *Gruppe*, made a good belly-landing at Hooe with a badly wounded *Bordfunker*. This 'D' variant carries 71/02 camouflage, with what appears to be a coat of primer on the lower fin and rudder painted carefully around the swastika. Undersurface colour (RLM 65) overspray is visible behind the fuselage code 'CB' to cover the original factory-applied code. The letter 'C' in the code is in the *Stab* colour of green. Note that the top of the letter 'C' is flat whereas the lower part is definitely curved. The W.Nr. 3339 was carried in white on the rear fuselage on the port side. This aircraft, together with W.Nr. 3341 in the next profile, was from the first batch of Bf 110s to be fitted with bomb racks and issued to the unit. Note in one of the photographs that the *Bordfunker*'s central rear canopy panel is missing, but not all of the frame has been removed. The unit emblem was carried on both sides of the forward fuselage. Koch and Kahl both survived into captivity. Kahl was so badly wounded that he was repatriated later in the war.

9 CB

Type: D-0/B
Period: Battle of Britain.
Unit: 2. *Staffel, Erprobungsgruppe* 210
Crew: *Oberleutnant* Alfred Habisch (pilot)
Unteroffizier Ernst Elfner (*Bordfunker*)

This aircraft, W.Nr. 3341, was one of a force of twenty-two from *Erprobungsgruppe* 210 that attacked Croydon (instead of the intended target, Kenley) airfield in the early evening of 15th August 1940. Intercepted by 32 and 111 Squadrons following the attack, the unit suffered the loss of seven aircraft: six Bf 110s and one Bf 109. After having received hits in the dogfight that followed the attack, the crew noticed that the tail section of the aircraft began to vibrate badly, and Habisch decided that it was more prudent to put down in England rather than chance a Channel crossing. He made an excellent belly-landing at Hawkhurst in Kent, both he and Elfner surviving into captivity. This Bf 110 was one of two German Messerschmitt aircraft shipped to the United States in 1941 for the U.S. aviation industry to evaluate. Its ultimate fate is not known, but it is almost certainly the most photographed Luftwaffe aircraft of World War II. It carried a top surface camouflage of 71/02, carried the unit emblem on the nose, and had one victory bar on the fin, claimed during the attacks on convoys during July 1940.

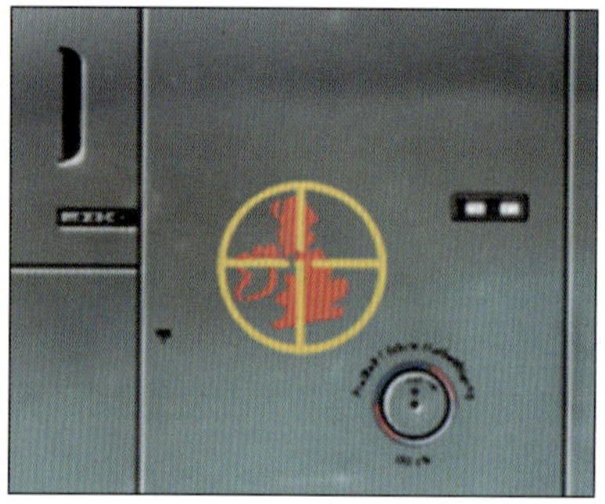

Right: Balthasar Aretz relaxes in flying gear and service cap.

Right: Formal portrait of Rolf Schilleng when a Gefreiter.

Type: D-0/B
Period: 21 August 1940, Battle of Britain.
Unit: 2./*Erprobungsgruppe* 210
Crew: *Unteroffizier* Balthasar Aretz (Pilot)
Gefreiter Rolf Schilleng (*Bordfunker*)

Aretz and Schilleng flew this aircraft during August 1940, the tailwheel collapsing on landing at Calais-Marck on 21st August 1940. In the photograph Rolf Schilleng leans against the rear fuselage. It has the extended rear fuselage common to the 'D' variant. Aretz favoured flying the 'E' of 2. *Staffel* whenever possible. The ultimate fate of this aircraft is not known. Upper surface camouflage is 71/02. The original four-character code on the fuselage has not been fully painted over, and is faintly visible in the photograph.

Type: D-0/B
Period: Battle of Britain.
Unit: 1. *Staffel*, *Erprobungsgruppe* 210
Crew: *Unteroffizier* Gerhard Rüger (pilot)
Gefreiter Edmund Ernst (*Bordfunker*)

A fighter-bomber from 1. *Staffel*, the two tone upper surface camouflage (71/02) is clearly evident. The *Staffel* use of the colour blue is also seen in the individual aircraft letter and the 'white-blue-white' of the propeller spinner. Of interest in the photograph is the dappled mottle on the fin and rudder of S9+PH, a Bf 110 C-6. S9+BH was shot down by P/O R. Dibnah of No.1 Squadron on 6 September 1940. Ernst baled out into captivity; Rüger was killed when the aircraft crashed.

Right: In this view of 1. Staffel aircrew relaxing in deck chairs, Gerhard Rüger is on the extreme left, with Edmund Ernst second from right in the striped deck chair. Franz Öllers is next to Ernst in the black deck chair.

Type: D-0/B
Period: Battle of Britain.
Unit: 1. *Staffel*, *Erprobungsgruppe* 210
Crew: *Leutnant* Ulrich *Freiherr* von der Horst (pilot)
Obergefreiter Franz Öllers (*Bordfunker*)

This 1. *Staffel* aircraft was shot down into the Channel on 24th September 1940 following a raid against the Spitfire works in Southampton, taking to their deaths von der Horst and Öllers. The aircraft carries the usual blue *Staffel* identity letter and distinctive white-blue-white propeller spinners. The W.Nr. 3384 was carried on the rear starboard fuselage. On the forward fuselage an emblem is seen. It would seem to be a tortoise/turtle in a light colour with a darker shell. The upper surface camouflage is 71/02, with a light application of 02 down the fuselage sides.

Left: Leutnant Ulrich Freiherr von der Horst stands between his Staffelkapitän, Martin Lutz (left), and an unknown member of 1. Staffel. Above: Portrait of Obergefreiter Franz Öllers, holding the rank of Gefreiter when the photograph was taken.

S9
HH

Type: D-0/B
Period: Battle of Britain.
Unit: 2. *Staffel*, *Erprobungsgruppe* 210
Crew: Not known.

Like other aircraft of the unit, the strong demarcation between the two upper surface camouflage colours can be seen. The photograph shows that the individual aircraft letter is clearly in a different colour to the rest of the fuselage code and the black central area of the fuselage cross, and it is therefore shown in the earlier 2. *Staffel* colour of red. It is likely, but by no means certain, that the aircraft in the photograph is S9+DK, W.Nr. 3370, that was 30% damaged following combat on 31st August 1940. *Feldwebel* Fritz Ebner (pilot), and *Gefreiter* Werner Zwick's S9+DK, shot down on the raid against the Parnall aircraft factory on 27th September 1940, carried the W.Nr.4270. From RAF Intelligence Reports the 'D'of their aircraft was black outlined in white. After combat damage Ebner made a good forced landing at Iwerne Minster with Werner Zwick badly wounded. Zwick was unconscious for several days and, following several operations, was repatriated in October 1943.

Type: D-3
Period: Battle of Britain.
Unit: *Gruppenstab*, *Erprobungsgruppe* 210
Crew: *Hauptmann* Martin Lutz (*Gruppenkommandeur*) (pilot)
Unteroffizier Anton Schön (*Bordfunker*)

On 27th September 1940, on a raid against the Parnall aircraft works at Yate, the nine Bf 110s of *Erprobungsgruppe* 210 were intercepted before they reached the target, and in the ensuing combat lost four aircraft. Among those shot down was the aircraft of Martin Lutz, the third *Gruppenkommandeur* of the unit, and Anton Schön. Their aircraft crashed at Tarrant Gunville and both Lutz and Schön were killed in the crash. Lutz's normal Bf 110, S9+AH, W.Nr.3371, had been damaged on landing some days earlier, so Lutz flew '+DH' as his replacement on the mission of 27th September. In the photograph the strong contrast between the two upper surface camouflage colours is evident. This aircraft also has the *Bordfunker*'s central rear canopy panel removed.

Right: Oberleutnant Martin Lutz, Staffelkapitän of 1. Staffel, Erprobungsgruppe 210, later third Gruppenkommandeur of that unit.

S9

Type: C
Period: Battle of Britain.
Unit: 8. *Staffel*, *Zerstörergeschwader* 26
Crew: Not known.

This crash-landed Bf 110 clearly has the short fuselage identifying it as a 'C' variant. It has the 'sad fox' emblem of 8. *Staffel* on the forward fuselage. Note the wide spacing between the characters of the unit code. The rear starboard fuselage carries the W.Nr. in white. The upper surface camouflage pattern is somewhat unusual in that the forward fuselage appears to carry a single, almost solid, camouflage colour, whereas aft of the letter 'S' the camouflage is lighter. This is no doubt due to the rear fuselage being repainted when the unit code was applied.

Type: C
Period: Battle of Britain.
Unit: 3. *Staffel*, *Zerstörergeschwader* 26
Crew: Not known.

This 'C' displays a mixture of styles. The early style solid upper surface camouflage is married to the late Battle of Britain period whitewashed nose, seen on many ZG 26 aircraft. Of interest is the small white band carried on the rear of the fuselage, the bolt-on armoured windscreen, and the lack of outline to the individual aircraft letter 'C'.

Type: C-1 (upgraded)
Period: Battle of Britain.
Unit: 3. *Staffel*, *Zerstörergeschwader* 26
Crew: Not known.

This C carries the white nose and thin white band around the rear fuselage, common to many aircraft of this unit in the later stages of the Battle of Britain. Note that the recess for 'parking' the rear machine gun has been faired over on this aircraft. The photograph shows the first style of radio mast on the lower port fuselage, and the early style canopy clearly lacking the D/F loop remote control on the canopy windscreen port side, common to the 'C-1' sub-variant. The rear central *Bordfunker*'s canopy panel is a revised and updated version; the original fitted to 'C-1's was fully enclosed and did not provide for the *Bordfunker*'s machine gun to be left in the firing position with the canopy fully closed. An armoured windscreen has also been fitted. All this points to a 'C-1' that has been upgraded with modifications common to later sub-variants.

Type: D
Period: Battle of Britain.
Unit: 7. *Staffel*, *Zerstörergeschwader* 26
Crew: Not known.

This 7. *Staffel* machine of ZG 26 differs from those shown previously of III. *Gruppe* by not having any tactical markings on the nose or rear of the aircraft. A yellow tactical marking can be seen on the lower part of the starboard rudder. This aircraft has an armoured windscreen and the rear machine gun recess faired over. The individual aircraft letter 'H' is white with no outline, and the spinner tips are in white, both features conforming to the use of the correct *Staffel* colour.

Type: D
Period: Battle of Britain.
Unit: 7. *Staffel*, *Zerstörergeschwader* 26
Crew: Not known.

This aircraft, unlike the previous profile, has a white nose. The W.Nr. appears on the rear fuselage. It has the extended rear fuselage housing a dinghy common to 'D' variants. Note the letter 'N' on the engine cowling, denoting the uprated DB 601N engine. This Bf 110 also has an armoured windscreen and the faired-over recess for the rear machine gun.

Type: C
Period: Battle of Britain.
Unit: 7. *Staffel*, *Zerstörergeschwader* 26
Crew: Not known.

Another 7. *Staffel* aircraft, once again displaying subtle differences to the previous profiles. Note where the white paint on the nose of the aircraft finishes. The short rear fuselage identifies this aircraft as a 'C' variant. Whereas the previous profile shows the W.Nr. on the rear fuselage, this Bf 110 has its W.Nr. high up on the fin. Compare the spacing of the characters of the unit code on this aircraft with those in the previous profile.

Type: C-4
Period: 25 September 1940
Unit: 7. *Staffel*, *Zerstörergeschwader* 26
Crew: *Oberleutnant* Ernst Matthes (*Staffelkapitän*) (Pilot)
Oberfeldwebel Franz Santel (*Bordfunker*)

On 25th September 1940 *Oberleutnant* Matthes led his 7. *Staffel* on an escort mission for KG 55 over the south-west area of England. Receiving damage in combat with Spitfires, Matthes managed to get back to France, bellying-in on one engine at Cherbourg in this aircraft, W.Nr.2130. Note again the area covered by white paint on the nose compared to previous profiles of this *Staffel*, and additionally the engine cowling painted white. Matthes's aircraft carried the *Staffel* emblem of a penguin carrying an umbrella, thought to be an oblique reference to the former British Prime Minister, Neville Chamberlain. It also had a large 'J' painted in white on the upper wing surface. The aircraft carries two victory bars on the fin, and the rudder marking appears to be the same shade as that seen on the fin upon which the two victory bars are painted. Also evident is the armoured windscreen. Matthes did not follow the normal practise of the *Staffelkapitän* flying aircraft 'A' in the *Staffel* up to this point in time, but subsequently flew 'A' for the rest of the year.

Type: C-4
Period: 27 September 1940
Unit: 8. *Staffel*, *Zerstörergeschwader* 26
Crew: *Unteroffizier* Fritz Schupp (Pilot)
Gefreiter Karl Nechwatel (*Bordfunker*)

This aircraft, W.Nr.3290, was attacked on 27th September 1940 by two Spitfires and such was the damage received that Schupp had to set it down near Kimmeridge, in Dorset. Both crewmen were wounded, but survived into captivity. Like previous profiles of III. *Gruppe*, *Zerstörergeschwader* 26 aircraft, this Bf 110 carries a yellow tactical marking on the rudder. In the RAF Intelligence report of the crashed aircraft, the individual aircraft letter 'D' was given as blue, unusual for an aircraft of this *Staffel*. The RAF Intelligence Report also mentions that yellow squares were found on the tailplane. The aircraft had red tips to the spinners, a white 'N' on the engine cowlings, denoting that it was powered by DB 601N engines, and an armoured windscreen. The three victory bars on the fin were for claims on 10th July and 18th July (two).

Type: C-2
Period: 27 September 1940
Unit: 15. *Staffel*, *Lehrgeschwader* 1
Crew: *Oberleutnant* Otto Weckeiser (Pilot)
Unteroffizier Horst Brüggow (*Bordfunker*)

This aircraft, shot down on 27th September 1940 at Oxted, Surrey after receiving hits in both engines, still carries the early style upper surface camouflage pattern and thin white outline to the fuselage cross. It had a white nose and yellow spinners. The unit emblem of a small wolf's head has been covered by the white tactical marking on the nose. The fin had four victory bars, for claims made on 13th August; 15th August (2) and 11th September. Windscreen armour was fitted. The individual aircraft letter of 'L' was yellow with no outline.

Type: E
Period: October 1940
Unit: 7. *Staffel*, *Zerstörergeschwader* 26
Crew: *Oberleutnant* Ernst Matthes (*Staffelkapitän*) (Pilot)
Oberfeldwebel Franz Santel (*Bordfunker*)

After crash-landing 3U+JR on 25th September 1940, *Staffelkapitän* Ernst Matthes took charge of Bf 110E, 3U+AR. This aircraft has a white nose with air inlet, armoured windscreen and the uprated DB 601N engines (the white 'N', denoting this engine, is clearly visible on the engine cowling). Note in the photograph the two faired-off areas under the wing that would normally accommodate underwing bomb racks. An indistinguishable W.Nr. can be seen on the rear fuselage.

Type: E
Period: Late 1940/1941
Unit: 5. *Staffel*, *Nachtjagdgeschwader* 1
Crew: Not known.

This nightfighter has the small inlet in the nose common to 'E' variant Bf 110s. The fuselage cross has a small white outline to the large black centre. The fuselage code appears to be in grey, and the aircraft carries a yellow fuselage band. Compare the placement of the fuselage band on 'L' with that on 'E' behind it. An armoured windscreen is fitted. Note that this aircraft has the upgraded 'scissors link' type tailwheel. Note also that the intake on the starboard fuselage for the cockpit heating system (just below the aerial connection point) is in the open position in the photograph.

Type: E
Period: 1941
Unit: 2. *Staffel*, *Zerstörergeschwader* 26
Crew: Not known.

This 'E' has the extended rear fuselage, a carry-over from the 'D' variant, and yellow engine cowlings. The yellow extends below the exhausts and back onto the next panel, as well as onto the propeller back plate and spinner. The I. *Gruppe* emblem is evident on the nose. This aircraft has no armoured windscreen. Of interest is the oversized letter 'K' in the unit code.

Type: D
Period: 1941
Unit: 6. *Staffel*, *Zerstörergeschwader* 76
Crew: *Oberfeldwebel* Spitzner
Bordfunker (not known)

This 'Sharksmouth' has a yellow nose cowling together with yellow engine cowlings, rudders and spinner tips. The propeller back plate also has a white section to it. The individual aircraft letter is in the *Staffel* colour of yellow with no apparent outline to it. The extended rear fuselage is evident in the photograph, in comparison to M8+AP that has the standard rear fuselage. Note how the undersurface blue overlaps onto the top of the port wing of M8+SP. An indistinguishable W.Nr. is carried on the rear fuselage.

Type: D
Period: 1941
Unit: 9. *Staffel*, *Zerstörergeschwader* 76
Crew: Not known.

This aircraft carries the full size '*Wespe*' emblem that later gained its greatest fame with *Zerstörergeschwader* 1 on the Russian front. This 'D' has the distinctive extended rear fuselage, and the rear fuselage, rudders and spinner tips in the *Staffel* colour of yellow. The individual aircraft letter of 'M' is in yellow with no outline, a practise that seems common to many *Zerstörer* aircraft. The cable running along the top of the fuselage can be clearly seen.

Type: D
Period: Spring 1941
Unit: 4. *Staffel*, *Zerstörergeschwader* 26
Crew: Not known.

This 'D' shown in the spring of 1941 during the Balkans campaign shows a couple of interesting features. The yellow fuselage band has, unusually, been painted over the fuselage code. Also, while the well-known ZG 26 clog emblem is carried, the ladybird emblem normally associated with III./ZG 26 is carried on a II. *Gruppe* machine. The possibility exists that this aircraft has been transferred from III. *Gruppe* to II. *Gruppe* without the emblem being removed. Yellow nose and rudders are evident, with the spinner tips being in the *Staffel* colour of white. The yellow on the nose is of a different shade to the yellow of the clog emblem. Note again the high demarcation line between the lower and upper surface camouflage colours on the port wing in the photograph. The white 'F' has no outline.

Type: C
Period: 1941
Unit: 3. *Staffel, Lehrgeschwader* 3
Crew: Not known.

This 'C', formerly of 15. *Staffel, Lehrgeschwader* 1, is shown in nightfighter camouflage of its new unit. Fuselage code is in grey, and an armoured windscreen has been fitted. The fuselage cross is white, requiring no further application against the black background.

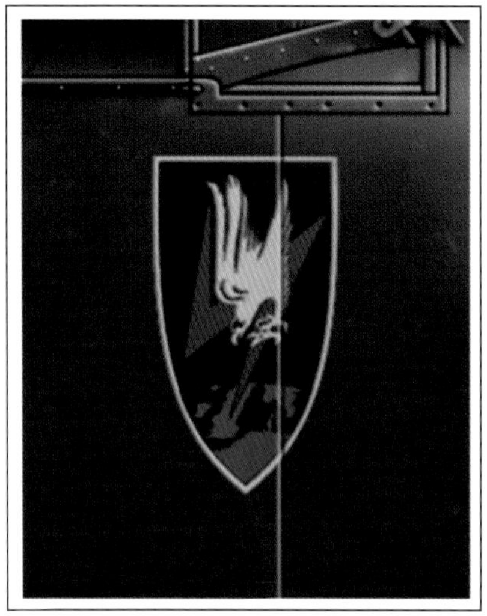

Type: D
Period: 1941
Unit: III. *Gruppe*, *Zerstörergeschwader* 26
Crew: Not known.

This III. *Gruppenstab* aircraft carries the ladybird in a diamond emblem seen in a previous profile on a II. *Gruppe* machine. It has yellow tactical markings on its extended rear fuselage and on the port rudder. The port engine cowling carries the letter 'N' denoting the uprated DB 601N engine. The individual aircraft letter and spinner tips are in the *Gruppenstab* colour of green. Note the bomb rack under the fuselage and the armoured windscreen.

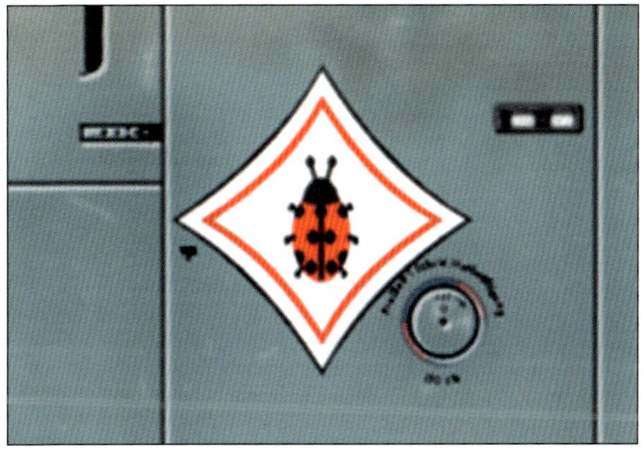

Type: E
Period: 1941
Unit: 4. *Staffel*, *Zerstörergeschwader* 26
Crew: Not known.

The inlet scoop on the nose can be seen in this photograph of a 1941 machine, identifying it as an 'E' variant. Of interest is the fact that the code letters either side of the fuselage cross are very close together. The letter 'G' is in white with no outline. The yellow fuselage band does not appear to extend beyond the bottom of the unit code of '3U'.

Type: E
Period: 1942
Unit: 7. *Staffel*, *Nachtjagdgeschwader* 4
Crew: Not known.

This 'E' is in the standard all black camouflage common to night fighters in the early years of night fighting, together with grey letters and numeral in the unit code. An armoured windscreen is fitted and supplementary fuel tanks are carried. The capped propeller spinner has a small ring on it in the *Staffel* colour of white. What is of particular interest on this machine are the two small attachments that can be seen: one under the nose, and the other under the number '3'. There is no recorded explanation as to what purpose they served. Note also that the undercarriage legs are painted black.

Type: E
Period: 1941
Unit: 4. *Staffel*, *Zerstörergeschwader* 26
Crew: Not known.

This 4. *Staffel* aircraft carries its unit code characters close together either side of the fuselage cross. Once again, in an aircraft of 4. *Staffel* of this unit, the yellow fuselage band appears to finish at the bottom of the fuselage code. Unlike 3U+GM, this Bf 110 of 4. *Staffel* has a black outline to its individual aircraft letter.

Type: D
Period: 1941
Unit: 7. *Staffel*, *Zerstörergeschwader* 26
Crew: Not known.

This III. *Gruppe* machine displays European theatre camouflage with the Mediterranean theatre fuselage band, in this case a very broad white band. The tip of the extended rear fuselage and the spinner tips are also painted white. The canopy has no armoured windscreen, and also has the *Bordfunker*'s central rear panel removed, as has been seen on previous profiles.

Type: D
Period: 1941
Unit: 7. *Staffel*, *Zerstörergeschwader* 26
Crew: Not known.

This 'D' displays a broad white fuselage band and white tip to the rear fuselage and spinners. However it carries the early-war solid camouflage down the sides of the fuselage. An armoured windscreen is fitted, and in the photograph the revised *Bordfunker*'s rear central canopy can be seen, with a cutaway to accommodate the permanent placement of the machine gun in a central position. The original 'parking place' for the machine gun on the top of the starboard fuselage has been faired-over. A single white victory bar is carried on the fin. The backplate to the spinners appears to be in a lighter colour than the rest of the spinners and engine cowlings, possibly RLM 02.

Type: D
Period: 1941
Unit: 9. *Staffel*, *Zerstörergeschwader* 26
Crew: Not known.

This 9. *Staffel* 'D' carries the cockerel *Staffel* emblem as well as the ladybird in a diamond emblem of III. *Gruppe*. A broad white theatre fuselage band is carried as well as a white tip to the rear of the extended fuselage. A yellow nose, yellow spinner tips and armoured windscreen can be seen, as can the W.Nr.3406, on the rear fuselage and 'N' on the engine cowling denoting the DB 601N engine. Underwing fuel tanks are in place. Three top surface colours are clearly evident, suggesting a 02/74/75/76 colour scheme. The yellow tactical marking on the rudder is to be seen, as in previous profiles of this *Gruppe*.

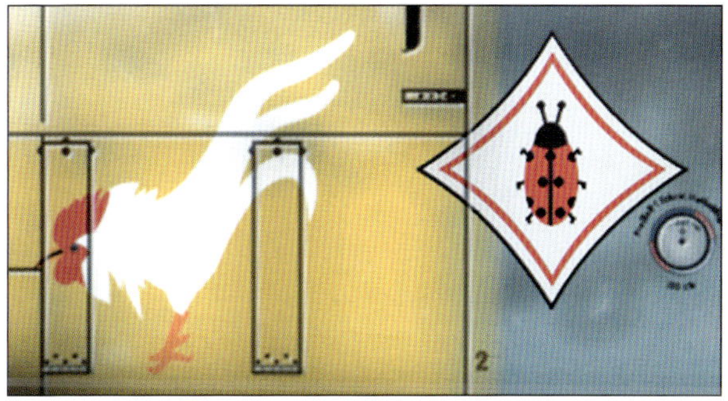

Type: E-3
Period: 1941
Unit: 1. *Staffel*, *Schnellkampfgeschwader* 210
Crew: Not known.

This E-3 was one of only a small batch of Bf 110s that were fitted with a rearward-firing MG 17 machine gun on each side of the fuselage and a 'periscope' (*Rückblickfernrohr* RF 1 A) fitted for the pilot's use. Available information states that about fifty aircraft were fitted with this combination as they passed through repair facilities, being redesignated 'E-3's. SD2 anti-personnel bombs are carried on the wing bomb racks. This aircraft carries the Russian front yellow theatre band on the forward fuselage, and an early-war style fuselage cross with a thin white outline to the central black cross. The photograph, however, does not show whether any unit emblem was carried on the nose of the aircraft.

Type: E-1
Period: 11th September 1941
Unit: 2. *Staffel*, *Schnellkampfgeschwader* 210
Crew: Not known.

This 'E' variant, which belly-landed near Seschtschinkaja after receiving combat damage, appears to have a light mottle down the sides of the fuselage. The emblem of *Erprobungsgruppe* 210 was carried forward into SKG 210, but was set in a white shield. This aircraft has an armoured windscreen and lacks the *Bordfunker*'s central rear canopy panel. The letters 'BK' on the fuselage appear to be larger than the unit code 'S9'. A yellow theatre band is carried ahead of the letter 'S' of the code. Two victory bars are on the port fin. The propeller back plates appear to be painted in black-green/white.

Type: E
Period: 1941
Unit: 1. *Staffel*, *Schnellkampfgeschwader* 210
Crew: Not known.

This crash-landed 'E' variant displays the yellow Russian front theatre fuselage band. The purpose of the darker area around the letters 'P' and 'H' of the fuselage code is not known, but it may be the case that previous letters have been crudely painted over. The photographs show evidence of three top surface camouflage colours, most likely 74/75/02. This is also evident on the starboard wing of the aircraft. The usual white/blue/white propeller spinners of 1. *Staffel* are carried, as is an armoured windscreen.

Type: E
Period: 1941
Unit: *Gruppenstab*, II. *Gruppe*, *Schnellkampfgeschwader* 210
Crew: Not known.

This 'E' variant in a very forlorn state has several interesting features. The fuselage cross appears to have been changed from the standard size prevalent in 1940 to one with a far greater black central area. The yellow fuselage band is in the early position of being between the unit code and the wing root. The channel for the rear fuselage cable release is clearly visible in the photograph, as is the armoured windscreen. Pilot's head armour can also be seen.

Type: C
Period: 1941/42
Unit: 7. *Staffel*, *Zerstörergeschwader* 26
Crew: Not known.

This Bf 110 with sand overall upper surfaces is a 'C', but it is difficult to establish the exact variant. It carries the early style aerial at the wing root (seen on the C-1, which changed with the change of radio on the 'C-2' variant), and the twin antennae attached to the cockpit mast. However the engine cowling does not have the small inlet seen only on the 'C-1' variant. It is likely, therefore, that this is a 'C-2' with an earlier radio system, or an upgraded 'C-1'. It carries white spinner tips, and the individual aircraft letter of 'J' is in fact just a black outline on the white theatre fuselage band. The configuration of the rear fuselage would tend to indicate that this aircraft was previously used in towing duties before being issued to ZG 26.

Type: E
Period: May 1941
Unit: 4. *Staffel*, *Zerstörergeschwader* 76
Crew: Not known.

4. *Staffel* was assigned to '*Sonderkommando Junck*' in May 1941 and transferred to Mosul in Iraq. The Bf 110s were repainted in Iraqi national markings for operations over that country. This machine is typical of the camouflage scheme carried on all of the *Staffel*'s aircraft. The Iraqi markings are on Luftwaffe-based camouflage with a white machine gun cowling and yellow engine cowlings. An armoured windscreen is fitted and an extended rear fuselage and air inlet on the nose can be seen.

Type: E-1
Period: May 1941
Unit: 4. *Staffel*, *Zerstörergeschwader* 76
Crew: Not known.

This aircraft, W.Nr.4035, was taken on charge by the RAF after it had belly landed near Mosul, Iraq. It acquired RAF markings, and after restoration to flying condition it was transferred to Egypt. After being flown by the RAF for several months it was finally written off after a belly landing in March 1942. This aircraft is famous for the words 'THE BELLE OF BERLIN' painted on its nose.

Type: E
Period: 1941/42
Unit: 7. *Staffel*, *Zerstörergeschwader* 26
Crew: Not known.

This 'E' carries the wide white theatre fuselage band, prevalent on several III./ZG 26 aircraft in the Mediterranean area, although European style camouflage is carried. A 75 litre oil tank can be seen under the fuselage. The *Staffel* emblem of a penguin carrying an umbrella is under the canopy, which has an armoured windscreen. Note the solid camouflage forward of the cockpit. Four white victory bars are carried on the fin.

Type: E
Period: 1941/42
Unit: 9. *Staffel*, *Nachtjagdgeschwader* 3
Crew: Not known.

Formed in November 1941 from 6. *Staffel*, *Zerstörer-geschwader* 76, this nightfighter sports the distinctive sharksmouth emblem of its previous unit. At this time of the war night fighter units were equipped with standard day fighter aircraft. This aircraft has an armoured windscreen and air inlet on the nose identifying it as an 'E' variant. Additionally, overall black camouflage is carried, with grey codes. Although the fuselage sides are painted black, the fuselage cross still has its centre painted black. The black centre of the cross had a slightly greater sheen to it than the black camouflage on the fuselage sides.

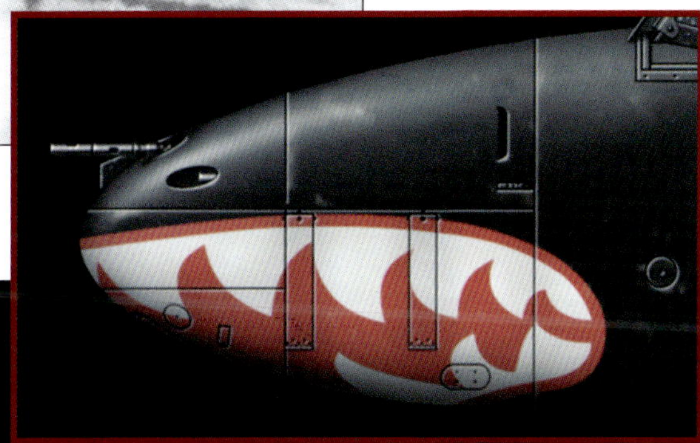

Type: F
Period: 1942
Unit: 9. *Staffel*, *Zerstörergeschwader* 26
Crew: Not known.

This abandoned 'F' variant carries the rarely seen individual aircraft letter of 'Z'. The yellow 'Z' carries no outline, and this aircraft has a yellow rudder and spinners. There is a clear demarcation between the two upper surface colours, and a third colour used on the fuselage side, the likely colours being 74/75/02. Note that the fuselage cross carries no black outline outside of the white areas. The *Bordfunker*'s rear canopy has no central panel, similar to earlier variants.

Type: E-1
Period: September 1941
Unit: 1.(Z) *Staffel*, *Jagdgeschwader* 77
Crew: *Lt.* Felix Brandis (Pilot)
Uffz. Alfred Harnach (*Bordfunker*)

On 1st September 1941 *Lt.* Brandis landed this E-1 at Tärendö in Sweden after following incorrect bearings. Heavily applied mottle is seen on the fuselage sides and fin and rudder, some of it straying onto the fuselage cross and swastika. This aircraft has an armoured windscreen fitted, carries eight victory bars on the fin and has the outer underside of the wing painted in yellow. The spinner is in black-green and white with a yellow tip. No individual aircraft letter is carried under the wing.

Type: D-0
Period: September 1941
Unit: 1.(Z), *Jagdgeschwader* 77
Crew: *Lt*. Felix Brandis (pilot)
Uffz. Guntram Weigl (*Bordfunker*)

Following his brief internment in Sweden, *Lt*. Brandis was soon flying missions again upon return to his unit. Flying this aircraft (normally the mount of *Ofw*. Munding) on a mission over enemy territory, he was hit in the left engine by flak and had to make a forced landing. LN+HR has the extended rear fuselage of the 'D' series, an armoured windscreen, and yellow tips to the spinners. In common with other aircraft of the *Staffel*, it would have the underside of the wingtips in yellow. Munding's two victory bars are seen on the fin.

Type: E
Period: 1941/42
Unit: 7. *Staffel*, *Zerstörergeschwader* 26
Crew: Not known.

Once again the wide white theatre band can be seen on this 7. *Staffel* 'E'. A 75 litre oil tank can be seen under the fuselage as well as underwing auxiliary fuel tanks. The *Bordfunker*'s central rear panel has been removed. The air inlet in the nose can be seen, but no extended rear fuselage. Although in the Mediterranean theatre, this aircraft carries European mottle style camouflage. Note that this aircraft has the short FuG 25 antenna under the central fuselage.

Type: E
Period: 1941/42
Unit: 6. *Staffel*, *Zerstörergeschwader* 26
Crew: Not known.

This 'E' carries the *Geschwader* emblem (the stylised 'Horst Wessel' letters on a red and black shield) as well as the white II. *Gruppe* clog carried on the engine cowling. The colour contrast between the fuselage cross and the fuselage band indicates that the band is yellow. The individual aircraft letter 'B' has a slightly different colour tone to it than the yellow fuselage band. An armoured windscreen can be seen, as can the air inlet on the nose. The spinner tips are white, when one would have expected them to be in the *Staffel* colour of yellow.

Type: E-2/Trop
Period: 1941/42
Unit: 8. *Staffel*, *Zerstörergeschwader* 26
Crew: Not known.

The remains of this Bf 110 made it somewhat difficult to determine the exact sub-variant of the machine, but reference to the excellent *Messerschmitt Bf 110/Me 210/ Me 410* book by Heinz Mankau and Peter Petrick leads us to the conclusion that it is an 'E-2/trop', and the colour profile has been constructed accordingly. The lack of an anti-roll bar in the cockpit behind the pilot's seat precludes this being an 'F' variant, and with the dust filter evident on the port wing and wing bomb racks inboard of the under wing cross, the conclusion is drawn that it is a tropicalised 'E'. Furthermore, information in Heinz and Peter's book points to the tropicalised 'E' variant having enlarged radiators, and this has been reflected in the profile. After close examination of the photograph, the conclusion is also drawn that the sand coloured camouflage extends around the whole of the fuselage. The undersurfaces of the wing have been shown in blue, common to that theatre's Luftwaffe aircraft. The 'G' is red, and the spinner tip is shown in red in accordance with common practise. An interesting aircraft, all the more so due to the detective work required that led to our conclusions.

Type: E-3
Period: 1942-1943
Unit: 2. *Staffel*, *Fernaufklärungsgruppe* 14
Crew: Not known.

This 'E-3' reconnaissance Bf 110 has been fitted with the tropical conversion kit. The enlarged radiator of this series can be seen on the lower engine cowling. A sand filter is evident on the port wing. An armoured windscreen is fitted, and the propellers are in white/black-green. Lightly mottled fins are contrasted with heavily mottled rudders. All four characters in the fuselage code are in black, and a white theatre band and stencilling on the fuselage can be clearly seen. The air inlet, first introduced on the 'E' series, is also to be seen on the nose cowling. The machine guns carry the protective 'sheaths' to prevent sand entering them prior to their firing.

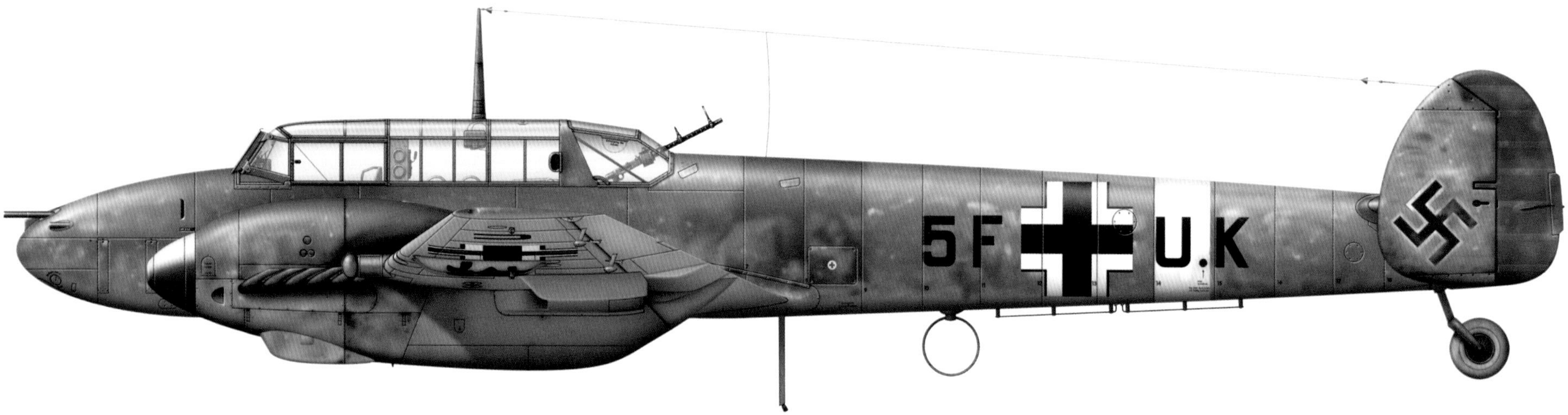

Type: C
Period: 1942
Unit: 1. *Staffel*, *Nachtjagdgeschwader* 3
Crew: Not known.

This 'C' carries an all-black camouflage apart from the fin, which is in a light shade of grey. A broad white rear fuselage band is carried, although this only covers the upper area of the fuselage. The fuselage code is in grey, with the individual aircraft letter 'D' outlined in white (which is repeated under the wing), and the spinner tips are in the *Staffel* colour of white. The fuselage cross is white outline only. The aircraft carries the large unit emblem of an owl on a crescent moon. An armoured windscreen is also in place.

Type: E
Period: Winter 1941/42
Unit: 4. *Staffel*, *Zerstörergeschwader* 1
Crew: Not known.

S9+AM, seen on the left of the photograph in the middle of a Russian winter, carries a light camouflage on its fuselage sides. The fuselage cross has a larger-than-normal black centre. The *Staffel* colour of white can be seen on the individual aircraft letter and on the spinner tips. The rudders have a darker mottle than the fin, and the yellow theatre band is carried aft of the wing root.

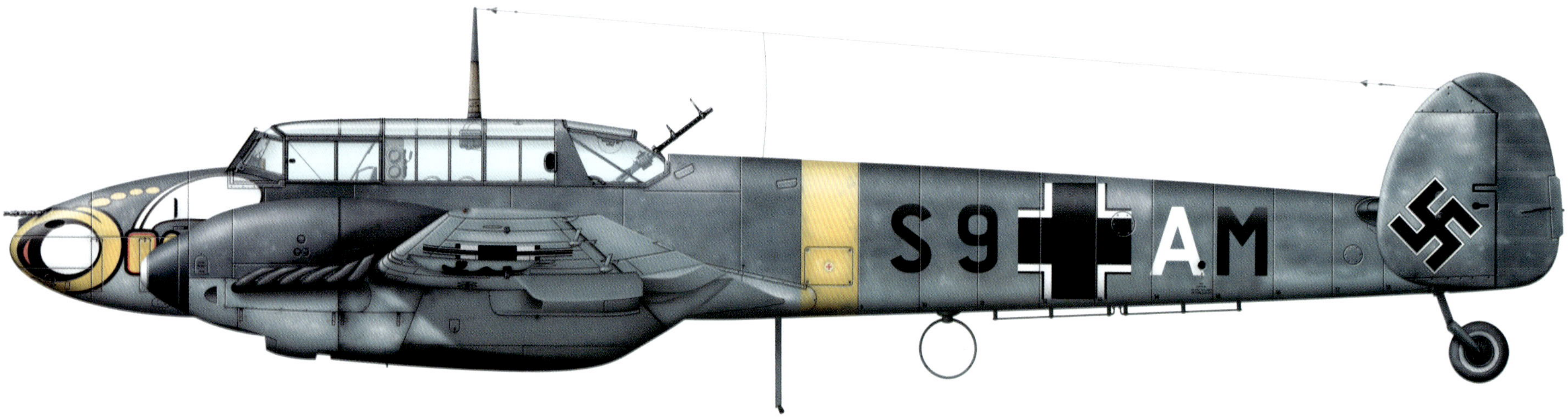

Type: E
Period: Winter 1941/42
Unit: 4. *Staffel*, *Zerstörergeschwader* 1
Crew: Not known.

This 'E', from the same photograph as the previous profile, shows identical positioning of the yellow theatre band, the distinctive '*Wespe*' on the nose and the white *Staffel* colour on the individual aircraft letter and spinner tips. However the fuselage cross is of the standard size, unlike the previous aircraft. An extended rear fuselage can also be seen.

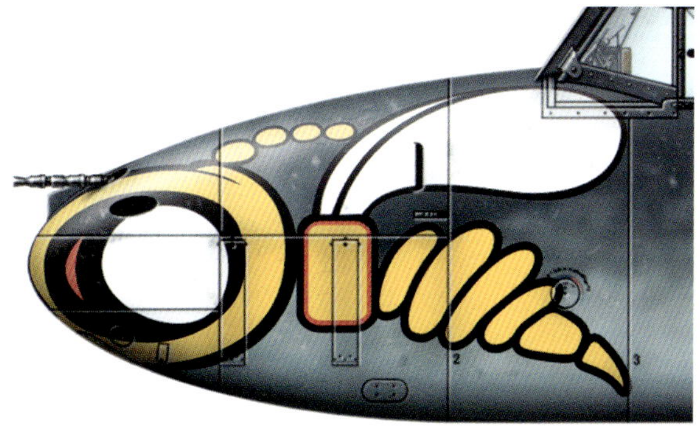

Type: E
Period: 1942
Unit: 4. *Staffel*, *Zerstörergeschwader* 1
Crew: Not known.

This 'E' of 1. *Staffel*, ZG 1 carries a standard-sized fuselage cross and the yellow theatre band just aft of the wing root, common to many aircraft of the unit. Points to note are the lack of the *Bordfunker*'s central rear canopy panel, and the top surface camouflage appearing high on the spine of the fuselage; the side mottling going almost right to the top. Note also the light area to the right of the letter 'F'. The white letter 'F' is thinly outlined in black. The 1. *Staffel* crew member on the left celebrating 100 missions is unknown; to the right is *Lt*. Manfred Theves, one time *Staffelkapitän* of 1. *Staffel*, who survived the war.

Type: C-7
Period: 1942
Unit: 6. *Staffel*, *Zerstörergeschwader* 1
Crew: Not known.

This Bf 110 does not have an air inlet on the nose and has a short rear fuselage, which precludes it being 'D' or 'E' variants. On 17th December 1942 Bf 110 C-7, S9+LP, W.Nr.3100, had both crew (pilot *Fw.* Alois Sonntag and *Bordfunker Uffz.* Christian Messner) wounded in action south of Ssulazki. The W.Nr. relates to a 'C-2' version, but it is known that earlier variants were repaired and re-designated as C-7s, fitted with bomb racks. This aircraft displays all the usual features of a ZG 1 aircraft of this period: the distinctive '*Wespe*' emblem; the yellow theatre band immediately aft of the wing root; the *Staffel* colour shown in the individual aircraft letter and on the spinner tips. A sand filter can be seen fitted to the port wing. An armoured windscreen is also fitted.

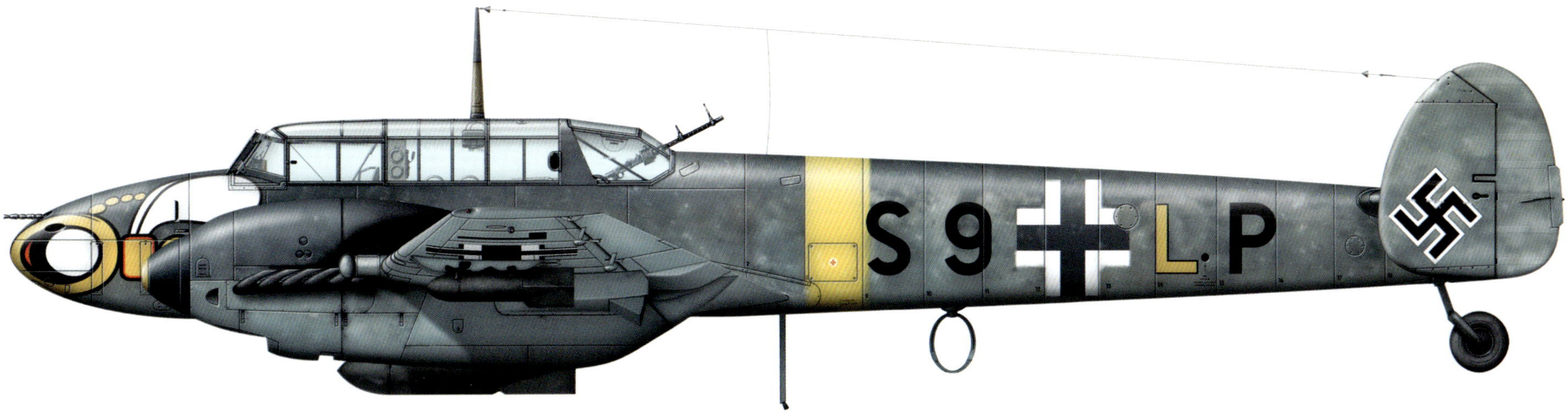

Type: F-2
Period: 1942
Unit: *Gruppenstab*, II. *Gruppe*, *Zerstörergeschwader* 1
Crew: Not known.

This 'F' displays some interesting features. The enlarged radiator and broader spinner point to this aircraft being an 'F'. Note also that this aircraft has a sand filter fitted to the port wing. An armoured windscreen is fitted, and the fin carries twenty victory bars. The only known pilots of the *Gruppenstab* of II./ZG 1 to have achieved at least twenty victories are Egon Albrecht, Rolf Kaldrack and Günther Tonne. The fuselage cross is notable for being of standard size but not having any black outline to the white area. The frame numbers on the lower fuselage are unusually prominent on this machine. The areas behind the codes 'S', '9' and 'C' show signs of overpainting before the application of these code letters and number. The individual aircraft letter, 'B', and the spinner tips are in the *Gruppenstab* colour of green. Whereas other aircraft of II. *Gruppe* carried the yellow theatre band just aft of the wing root, this aircraft has its theatre band on the rear of the fuselage. The undersides of the wing tips were also painted yellow. Note that the letter on the underside of the wing is 'G', not 'B'. It is also worth noting the slight variation in the '*Wespe*' emblem compared to other aircraft of ZG 1. Close examination of this emblem, in fact, shows many minute variations of the same theme.

Type: 'E'
Period: 1942
Unit: 5. *Staffel*, *Zerstörergeschwader* 1
Crew: Not known.

This aircraft has the extended rear fuselage and air inlet on the nose seen on the 'E' variant. Interestingly, the top surface camouflage on the spine of the fuselage shows a lighter colour than on the fuselage sides, as does the wings. There is also another variation on the placement of the yellow Russian front theatre band, behind the individual aircraft letter, which is in the early war *Staffel* colour of red. The spinner tips are also in this colour. Note that the yellow theatre band does not extend completely around the fuselage, but stops at the bottom of the letter 'D'.

Type: E
Period: 1942
Unit: 5. *Staffel*, *Zerstörergeschwader* 1
Crew: Not known.

This 'E' has an armoured windscreen, air inlet on the nose, but does not have the extended rear fuselage. The letter 'T' is red with a thin black outline, and the central dark colour of the fuselage cross is lighter than the three black characters of the fuselage code. The yellow theatre band is in the more usual position for II./ZG 1, aft of the wing root. Note that the lower white areas of the fuselage cross have a slight fuselage camouflage overspray on them.

Type: 'D'
Period: 1942
Unit: 3. *Staffel*, *Zerstörergeschwader* 1
Crew: Not known.

This nosed-over 'D' shows certain variations from other profiles of '*Wespe*' aircraft. Whereas the Russian theatre band is aft of the wing root, the first letter of the fuselage code is on the yellow band, thereby moving forward the code and fuselage cross from the more normal placement. The *Staffel* colour of yellow covers all but the spinner back plate, rather than just the spinner tip, more normally seen. The extended rear fuselage is evident, as is the lack of the *Bordfunker*'s central rear panel. The style of the wasp's wing is also different from that normally seen on aircraft of ZG 1.

Type: E-1
Period: 13th July 1942
Unit: 5. *Staffel*, *Zerstörergeschwader* 1
Crew: *Ofw*. Willi Dibowski (pilot)
Uffz. Kurt Meier (*Bordfunker*)

Willi Dibowski belly-landed this 'E' near Woroschilowgrad following a hit from flak while attacking Russian tanks. The yellow fuselage band is in a different position to the following profile, and the W.Nr.4054, unusually is on the top of the fin rather than the more conventional position of on the rear fuselage. Note that the top of the 'S' is flat, as opposed to a curve on the lower part of the letter. Again, this aircraft of the '*Wespe*' unit carries a very light colour on the fuselage spine. Both Dibowski (left, in the photograph with Meier) and Meier survived the war.

Type: E
Period: August 1942
Unit: 5. *Staffel*, *Zerstörergeschwader* 1
Crew: Not known.

This 'E', seen at Kuteinikowo in August 1942, appears to be on standby for take-off, with the pilot and *Bordfunker* in position and a member of groundcrew on the port engine. The *Bordfunker*'s machine gun is centrally sited, with the central canopy panel removed. Note the solid camouflage on the port engine cowling. The spine of the fuselage carries a very light camouflage colour. This can also be seen on the wing camouflage of the photographing aircraft. A III./ZG 1 Bf 109E can be seen in the distance in the photograph.

Type: D
Period: 1942
Unit: 8. *Staffel*, *Nachtjagdgeschwader* 4
Crew: Not known.

This 'D' is in the little-seen camouflage of light blue overall. The canopy framing is in a darker colour, almost certainly that of the original camouflage applied to it. An armoured windscreen is fitted. Note the camouflage overspray on the nightfighter emblem, and also on the top right area of the fuselage cross, which carries no black outline to the white sections of the cross. The revised rear wheel with the 'scissors link' is also fitted.

Type: E-2/U-1
Period: September 1942
Unit: 5. *Staffel*, *Zerstörergeschwader* 1
Crew: *Unteroffizier* Gottfried Seifert (Pilot)
Unteroffizier Alfred Brandt (*Bordfunker*)

Photographed early in September 1942 at Armawir, this E-2/U-1, S9+UN, W.Nr.2542, was listed missing in action on 17th September 1942 after it was rammed by a Russian fighter fifteen kilometres east of Ischerskaja. The 'U-1' denotes a Bf 110 deployed on towing duties and there are identifying features in the photograph that points to this being one of them. This 'E' carries the enlarged radiator, more commonly seen on the 'F' series that was fitted to 'E' series aircraft on towing duties. Additionally, the rear section of the fuselage is missing on the aircraft in the photograph, another feature of a towing Bf 110 in order to accommodate the cable mechanism. These features can be seen in the later profile of 2S+EL. When Bf 110s were no longer required for towing duties, they were allocated to front-line units, and this is the likely situation with this aircraft.

Type: E-2/Trop
Period: 1941/42
Unit: 7. *Staffel*, *Zerstörergeschwader* 26
Crew: Not known.

This 'E' has sand overall top surfaces with white theatre band on the rear fuselage. The spacing between the '3' and the 'U' is wider than that between the 'O' and 'R', apparently to fit the latter two letters on the white theatre band. The 'O' needs only to be in black outline on the white band in order to comply with the *Staffel* colour of white. An auxiliary fuel tank is evident under the port wing, and an indistinguishable W.Nr. is on the port fin. According to published sources, the lack of an anti-roll bar behind the pilot points to this being an 'E' variant, and the larger radiator would be accompanied by sand filters for the engines. Note also the FuG 25 antenna under the central fuselage.

Type: F-2
Period: Winter 1942/43
Unit: 10.(Z) *Staffel*, *Zerstörergeschwader* 5
Crew: Not known.

This 'F-2' carries white winter camouflage that is beginning to show signs of wear. The rudders and underwingtips are painted yellow. An auxiliary fuel tank can be seen under the starboard wing and the individual aircraft letter, 'F' is outboard of the wing cross on the yellow area. The later-style pitot tube can also be seen under the starboard wing.

Type: E-1/U-1
Period: 1942
Unit: 3. *Staffel*, *Zerstörergeschwader* 2
Crew: Not known.

This aircraft shows the modifications made to convert it to a towing aircraft for Me 321 gliders. A rear view mirror can be seen ahead of the armoured windscreen; the rear fuselage section has been removed to accommodate the towing equipment; the cable route along the lower fuselage is clearly evident, and enlarged radiator cowlings have been fitted, more commonly seen on the 'F' and 'G' series. The clog emblem on the engine cowling would indicate that at one time this aircraft served with ZG 26, although the fuselage code definitely shows the unit code '2S' of ZG 2. Of interest, in connection with ZG 26, is the yellow marking on part of the rudder, which is also in evidence on some of the earlier ZG 26 profiles. Note once again the very light camouflage on the spines of both aircraft.

Type: F-2/Trop
Period: Summer 1942
Unit: 13.(Z)/*Jagdgeschwader* 5
Crew: Not known.

'F' variants were on charge with JG 5 from at least May 1942, and this aircraft is indicative of the features to be found on aircraft of the unit from mid-1942 onwards. The fuselage code is in black, with the individual aircraft letter outlined in white. Camouflage on the fuselage sides appears to be lighter than on previous profiles of 'D' and 'E' variants of the unit. The larger radiator can clearly be seen, as can the armoured windscreen and tropical filter. Spinner tips are white and, in common with other aircraft of this unit, the undersurface wingtips are painted yellow. The famous emblem of this unit, a Rata in the jaws of a Dackel, is also carried.

Type: F-2
Period: Winter 1942/43
Unit: 13.(Z)/*Jagdgeschwader* 5
Crew: Not known.

This F-2, in the classic '*kopfstand*' position, was photographed at Kemijärvi in mid-winter. White winter camouflage has been applied, not in a solid application, but in a rather exotic fashion. Three characters of the fuselage code have been overpainted, but not obscured; the third character, individual aircraft letter 'R', has been left untouched or re-applied after the application of the winter camouflage. The 'F' series engine is evident, with the enlarged radiator and bigger, rounded spinner. An armoured windscreen was fitted, and the undersurface wingtips are painted yellow, with the individual aircraft letter painted on the yellow section. The standard sized fuselage cross carries no black outline.

Type: E
Period: 1942
Unit: 1. *Staffel*, *Zerstörergeschwader* 1
Crew: Not known.

This 'E' does not have an armoured windscreen but is fitted with the larger radiator more usually seen on later variants, and a propeller spinner of the type seen on the 'C' to 'E' series. It is therefore likely that this was an 'E-2/Trop variant, the enlarged radiator being coupled with tropical fittings. Note that a three-colour top surface camouflage is in evidence, with the two darker shades forward of the cockpit, and the lighter shade in the area of the '9' of the unit code. It would appear that the SKG 210 emblem was not on the aircraft, but added later in the photo laboratory. A colour view of this aircraft (taken by PK photographer Markward) shows a photograph of this aircraft retouched to show a code of S9+BH!

Type: 'D'
Period: 1942
Unit: II./*Zerstörer Schule* 1
Crew: Not known.

This 'D' carries what appears to be an old fuselage code beneath the cockpit. The extended rear fuselage and armoured windscreen can be seen. A number, commonly found on training aircraft, and a yellow fuselage band, are carried aft of the fuselage cross.

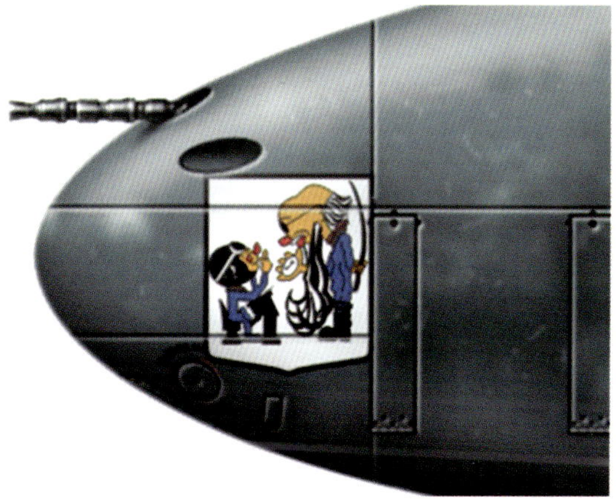

Type: G-2
Period: 1943
Unit: 5. *Staffel*, *Zerstörergeschwader* 1
Crew: Not known.

This G-2 operated out of Montecorvino in 1943. It is fitted with an armoured windscreen and sand filter. The large propeller boss associated with the 'G' variant can clearly be seen. Note the fuselage cross does not have a black outline surrounding the white area. The rear fuselage band also overlaps the *Staffel* letter slightly. Although bomb racks are evident under the wing, no individual aircraft letter is carried there. This aircraft had the revised sideways-opening rear *Bordfunker*'s canopy fitted.

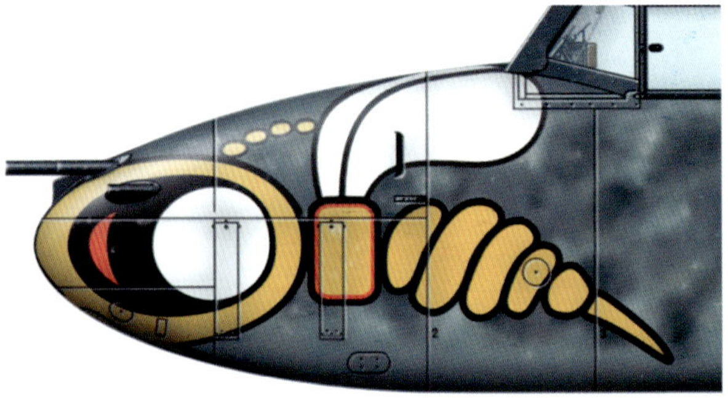

Type: G-2
Period: 1943
Unit: 1. *Staffel*, *Zerstörergeschwader* 1
Crew: Not known.

This G-2 has the revised sideways-opening rear *Bordfunker*'s canopy. The standard bomb racks under the wing and central fuselage, coupled with standard armament and yellow fuselage band would indicate that this aircraft operated on the Russian Front, rather than against USAAF bombers, when the forward firing armament was beefed up considerably. An armoured windscreen is fitted.

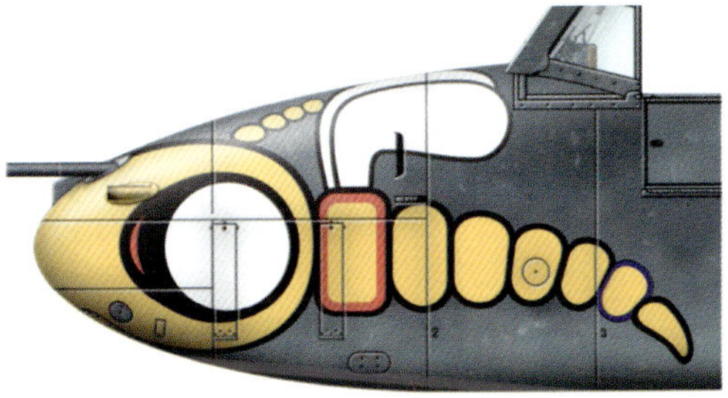

Type: G-2/R-2
Period: 1944
Unit: 4. *Staffel*, *Zerstörergeschwader* 76
Crew: Not known.

The 37mm *Kanone* was fitted to many G-2 day fighters to provide a greater weight of fire against the USAAF day bombers. This aircraft also carries the 'M5' modification pack: two *Nebelwerfer* 21cm mortars beneath each wing. Additionally, the GM 1 nitrous oxide system to boost high altitude engine performance was fitted to some Bf 110s. This necessitated the removal of the rear-firing gun and armour in that area of the aircraft to accommodate the cylinder housing the nitrous oxide. This G-2 clearly shows the lack of rear firing gun and is no doubt an 'R-2' sub-variant. The unit code 'M8' is of the reduced-size style prevalent in the later years of the war. The fuselage cross contains no black outline to the white area, and a wide yellow fuselage band is carried aft of the unit code.

Type: G-2
Period: 1944
Unit: 3. *Staffel*, *Zerstörergeschwader* 26
Crew: Not known.

This G-2 displays the later, well-known, sideways opening canopy for the *Bordfunker*. Yellow '6' and spinners conform to 3. *Staffel* colouring. A supplementary fuel tank can be seen under the wing. There is no black outline to the white area of the fuselage cross, and the rear of the aircraft carries a broad white fuselage band. Note the 'white outline only' style of fuselage cross on 'Yellow 2'.

Type: G-2
Period: 1944
Unit: 5. *Staffel*, *Zerstörergeschwader* 1
Crew: Not known.

This G-2 carries two MG 151/20 in a ventral housing, as well as two further MG 151/20 in the upper nose. An armoured windscreen is fitted and the aircraft carries supplementary fuel tanks under the wings. The individual aircraft letter of 'L' is in the *Staffel* colour of red, and the last two letters of the fuselage code are on a wide yellow fuselage band, these two colours also appearing on the propeller spinners.

Type: G-4
Period: 1943
Unit: 9. *Staffel*, *Nachtjagdgeschwader* 3
Crew: Not known.

This G-4 night fighter carries FuG 202 'Lichtenstein BC' radar and is camouflaged in the more usual mid-to-late war scheme of greys. Flame dampers are fitted to the exhaust stubs, and bomb racks are fitted under the wings. The earlier style rudder is evident in the photograph on the starboard side. The pitot tube is in the wing inboard position, more normally associated with earlier versions, but also seen on early 'G' versions. All the foregoing points to this being from an early batch of 'G's, perhaps a converted 'G-2' day fighter, given the features more normally in evidence on that variant.

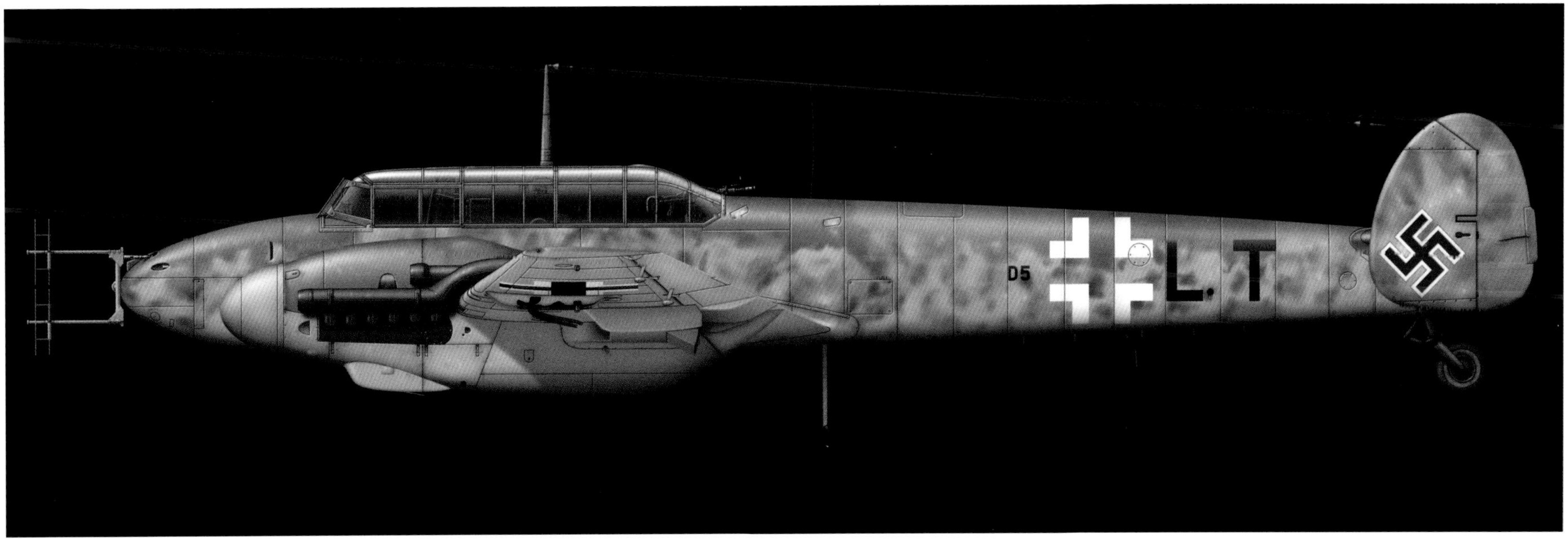

Type: G-2
Period: 1943
Unit: 5. *Staffel*, *Nachtjagdgeschwader* 200
Crew: Not known.

This unit operated principally on the Eastern Front in the night fighting role. This G-2 displays the MG 81Z twin guns in the *Bordfunker* position coupled with the later style sideway-opening *Bordfunker*'s rear canopy. Auxiliary fuel tanks are carried beneath the wings. The unit code, '8V', is in the later-war style of small characters, and the individual aircraft letter 'M' is red, a return to the pre- and early-war practise of 2., 5. and 8. *Staffeln* colour, which was later replaced by black. A yellow fuselage band is carried, and the standard size fuselage cross does not have a black outline. A 57mm armoured windscreen is fitted. Note the football pitch markings on the ground in the photograph.

Type: G-2
Period: 1943
Unit: 5. *Staffel*, *Nachtjagdgeschwader* 200
Crew: Not known.

From the same *Staffel* as the previous profile, this 'G-2' shows heavier mottling on the fin and rudder, and the fuselage cross does not have a black centre, but is simply broad white outline. This aircraft also carries the later-style canopy and MG 81Z *Bordfunker*'s armament. Spinner tips are in the *Staffel* colour of red.

Type: G-4
Period: April/May 1944
Unit: 5. *Staffel*, *Nachtjagdgeschwader* 5
Crew: *Oberleutnant* Wilhelm Johnen (Pilot)
Bordfunker not known.

Oberleutnant Johnen landed this G-4 at Dübendorf in Switzerland on 28th April 1944. The profile shows the aircraft as it is seen in most photographs, with armament removed. FuG 220 SN-2 and FuG 212 radar aerials are in evident in the nose. FuG 25 and FuG 16ZY aerials were fitted. The camouflage consists of two-tone grey: close curly mottle over a darker base grey. The fuselage code is in black with a white outline only fuselage cross. An armoured windscreen, exhaust flame dampers and auxiliary fuel tanks are fitted. Seventeen victory bars are carried on the port fin.

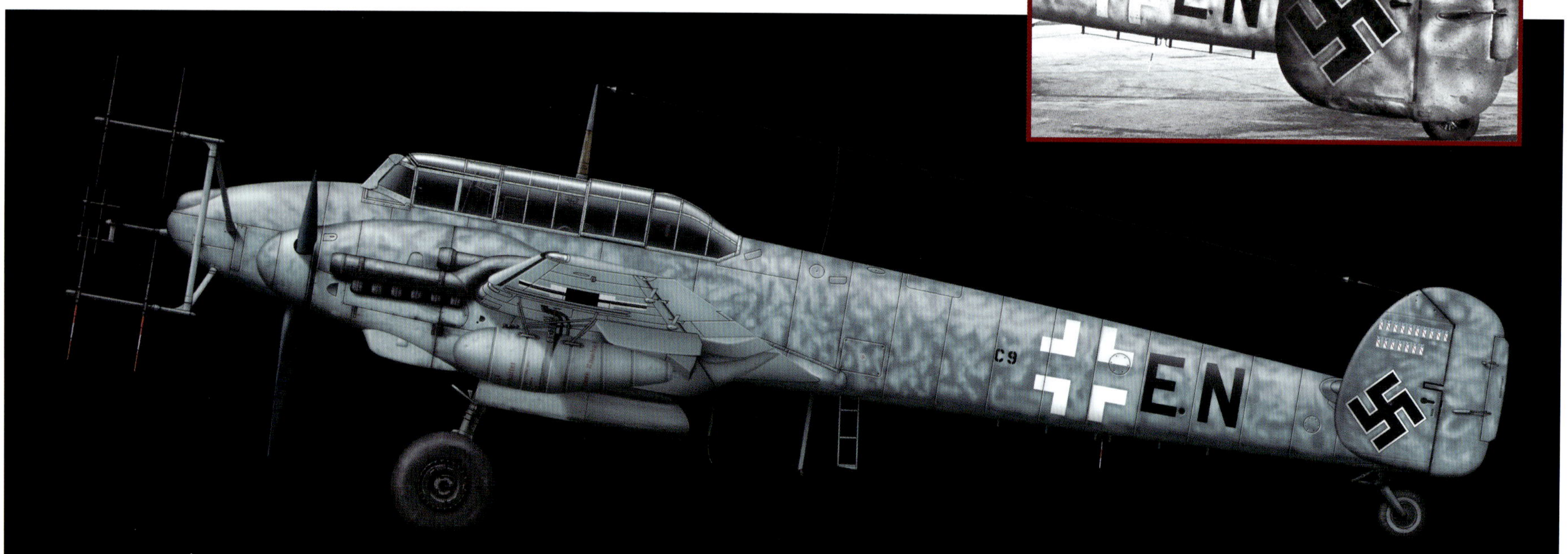

Type: G-2
Period: Winter 1943/44
Unit: 5. *Staffel*, *Zerstörergeschwader* 1
Crew: Not known.

This aircraft displays many of the features commonly seen on the G-2. The later-style sideways opening canopy, together with the MG 81Z rearward firing armament for the *Bordfunker*, are fitted. An armoured windscreen, 21cm mortar tubes, and auxiliary fuel tanks under the wing can also be seen. The 'M1' pack of two 151/20 20mm cannons is also installed under the forward fuselage. The individual aircraft letter 'M' is in the *Staffel* colour of red, as are the spinner tips. The reduced size unit code, 2N, can be seen on the broad white fuselage band. The fuselage cross is standard size but without the outer black outline.

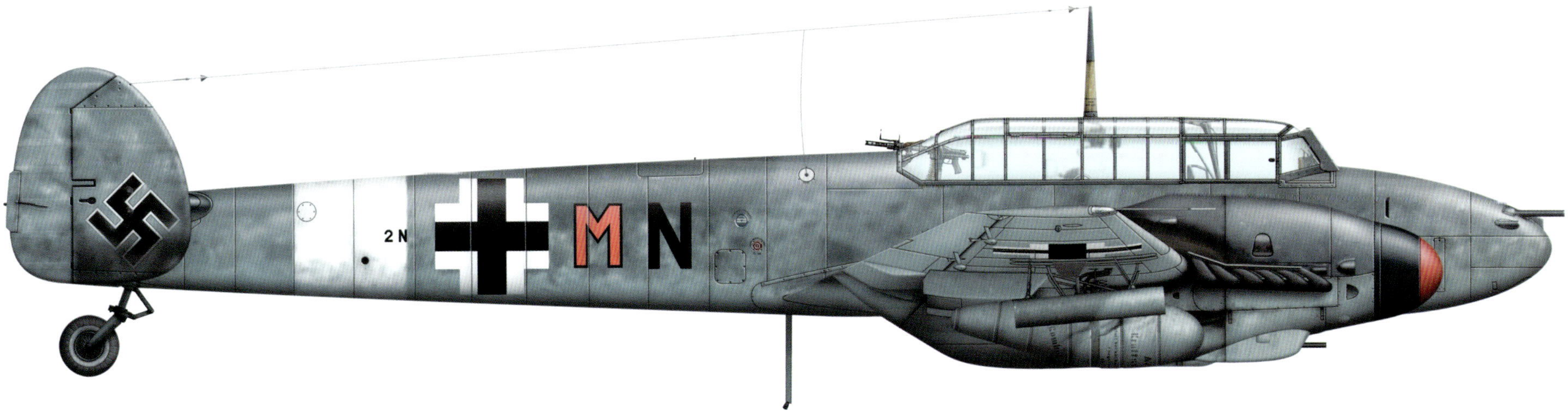

Type: G-4
Period: 1944/45
Unit: *Gruppenstab, Nachtjagdgeschwader* 1
Crew: *Major* Martin Drewes
(pilot) *Gruppenkommandeur*)
Oberfeldwebel Erich Handke (*Bordfunker*)
Oberfeldwebel Georg Petz (*Bordschutze*)

Martin Drewes, as *Gruppenkommandeur*, had at his disposal two Bf 110 Gs, one for night fighting, and another for daylight missions. Unusually, he used a G-4, normally the night fighter variant, on daytime interception missions. This aircraft, his daytime mount, carries twenty-two victory bars and reference to his award of the Knight's Cross, which would date the photograph post-27th July 1944. Camouflage is very light, and small unit letters, prevalent for all units in the latter stages of the war, are carried. To achieve greater speed, Drewes had his aircraft polished, and any heavy armour plate taken out. Martin Drewes had six day victories among his final tally of forty-nine.

Appendix
Messerschmitt Bf 110 Variants

The images in this appendix are general views of the main and most produced versions of the *Zerstörer*. Note that pictorial evidence shows that on the change from one variant to another, new variant aircraft were often constructed with parts that were standard on the previous variant. Many were retrofitted and upgraded in the field, and it was not uncommon to see a previous version with subsequent improvements. This was particularly true for G series aircraft, with several combinations of antennae and armament seen on operational aircraft.

Bf 110B

Profile 1

The very first Bf 110 production aircraft could be seen unarmed (usually in the Training Schools) and with a full complement of armament with service units. The Jumo 210 engine cowlings are immediately recognizable on the Bf 110B. Together with the main, larger radiator, both cowlings had a large air scoop on the right hand side, and a small one on the left. Two other air intakes were under the wing. The tail wheel had a diameter of 350mm, and the main wheel hubcaps had a six-spoked structure. The wings had a rounded tip.

Profile 2

The *Bordfunker*'s rear canopy was fully enclosed. This meant that the rear canopy had to be opened in order to swing the rearward-firing machine gun into the firing position. The rear moveable part of the canopy had a small half rounded access hatch on the left. The gunner usually held the handgrip with his left hand, and accessed its lock with his right hand. Spinners on the 'B' variant had a rounded cap.

Profile 3

Profile 4
The MG 17s in the upper nose of the Bf 110 protruded by different lengths through the cowling, due to the staggered placement of them in the nose. The upper MG on the starboard side had a rectangular gap, due to the need to accommodate the machine gun's support arm.

Bf 110C

Profile 5
The first sub-variant was the C-1. The most obvious difference to the 'B' version was the upgrade to DB 601A engines that significantly changed the entire engine cowling and exhausts layout.

Profile 6
The canopy had its frame design refined and the structure of the middle section was slightly changed. The three perspex centre panels in the canopy were now the same size.

Profile 7
The rounded spinner caps were replaced by an open cap. New radiators appeared under the wing. They would remain in the same position right through to the last variant.

Profile 8
Wing tips changed from rounded to square tips. The navigation lights were moved forward.

Profile 9
On C-2 aircraft, the small air intake on the left of the engines was removed, giving place to another air intake just ahead the exhausts. The underbelly mast next to the small ladder on the port side of the fuselage was changed for a slimmer, more vertical version. It had a cable inside attached to ballast that allowed it to be extended by the radio operator. In the left side of the cockpit, behind the pilot, the remote control for the D/F loop antenna was moved from the cockpit floor to a position on the port side of the canopy.

Profile 10
The wing root fairings received a riveted thin sheet as reinforcement. Due to the change of radio equipment (replacement of the FuG IIIaU with the FuG X), both isolators were removed from the fuselage and the portside aerial was deleted. The position of some of the radio operator's instruments was changed, being housed in a folded metal sheet just behind the pilot's shoulders. The main wheel's diameter was increased from 815 to 875mm, with a new layout for the hubcap. The tail wheel had its diameter increased to 380mm.

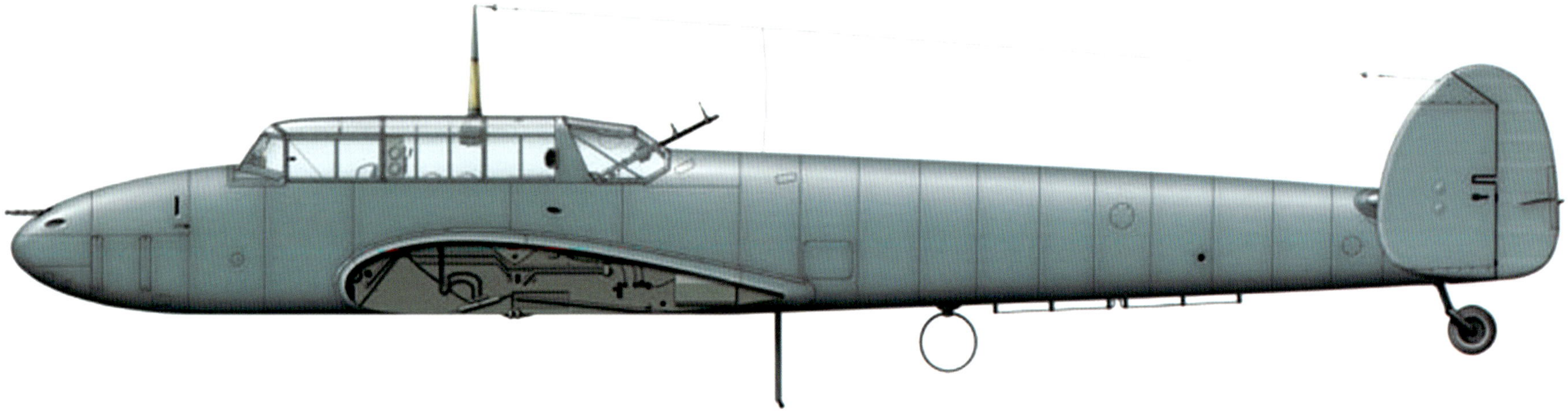

Profile 11
C-3/4 aircraft had the MGFF underbelly cannon replaced by the MGFF 'M' and the underbelly bulge (*Hülsenwanne*), a necessity to accommodate the earlier 20mm ammunition drums, disappeared.

Profile 12

With a revised *Bordfunker*'s rear central canopy that had an opening to allow for the permanent placement of the MG 15, the need for a starboard side trough to 'park' the MG 15 was no longer required, and photographs show that Bf 110s started to be fitted with a small plate covering the trough to make the fuselage more streamlined. With this change, the *Bordfunker* could operate the machine gun with the rear canopy fully closed. Some units, particularly *Erprobungsgruppe* 210, seemed to favour removing the rear central canopy completely. It is not known whether this was for reasons of easier firing of the machine gun, or as an easier means of escape for the *Bordfunker* in a baling-out situation. Whatever the reason, many aircraft can be seen with this panel missing from the 'C' series onwards. The C-5 was a purely reconnaissance version, having its two 20mm MGFF 'M' cannons removed and an RB 50/30 camera fitted in their place.

Profile 13

Profile 14

Profile 15
C-6 aircraft had a 30mm MG 101 installed in place of the two 20mm cannons. This was a factory modification, and ultimately only twelve were ever built.

Profile 16
C-7 aircraft were earlier C variants that were repaired/modified and brought up to fighter-bomber standard, receiving ETC bomb racks. They retained their W.Nr., and the profile of S9+LP shows one such aircraft, having a 'C-2' W.Nr., but definitely identified in Luftwaffe Loss Lists as a 'C-7'.

Bf 110D

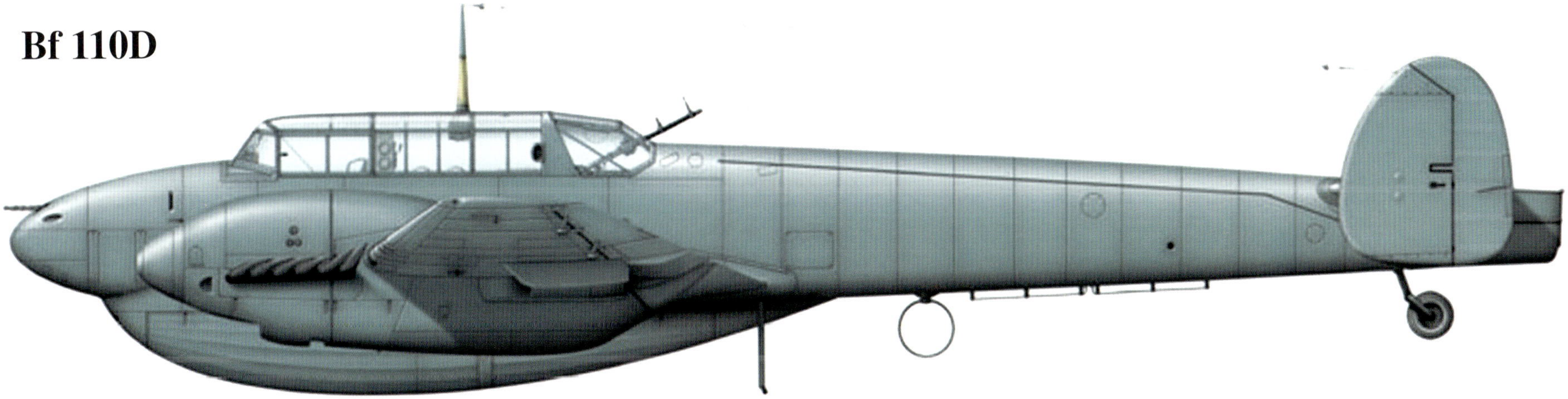

Profile 17
The first D-0 series aircraft were slated to receive a 106 litre underbelly fuel tank (*Dackelbauch*). However a certain amount of confusion has reigned regarding the 'D' series designations.

Profile 18
The D-0 was indeed a *Dackelbauch* version, but the factories also produced the D-0/B fighter-bomber version, the first batch being issued to the fighter-bomber unit Erprobungsgruppe 210 upon its formation on 1st July 1940.

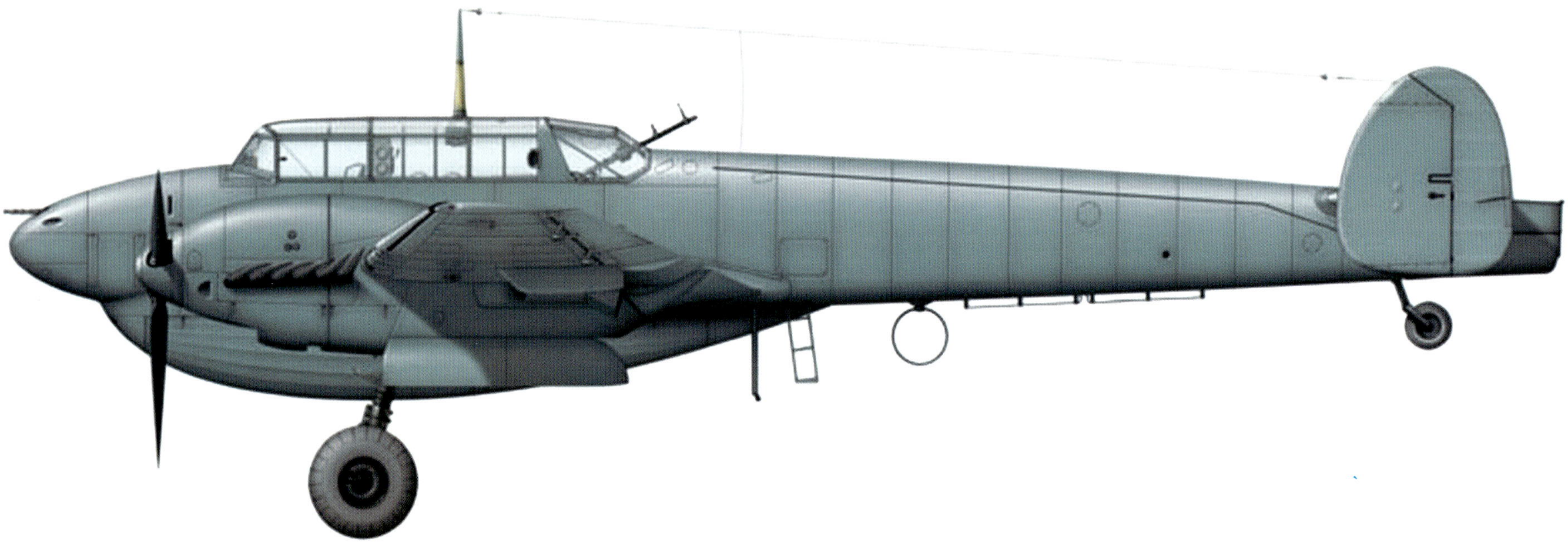

Profile 19
These aircraft carried the extended rear fuselage housing a dinghy and emergency equipment and articles. In the event of an emergency water-landing, the tail cone could be opened by a latch operated by the *Bordfunker*. Upon being released the tail cone opened about a hinge at the rear and released the life raft. A thin cable held in clips along the outside of the top of the fuselage provided for the raft to be pulled forward to the crew.

Profile 20
The D-1 series, of which very few were produced, was to have no *Dackelbauch*, but auxiliary tanks under the wings to increase the aircraft's range.

Profile 21
The D-2 sub-variant was to be capable of being fitted with either a *Dackelbauch* or bomb racks under the fuselage. Photographs exist showing Bf 110s of the 1940 period with the *Dackelbauch* rivet lines while fitted with bomb racks.

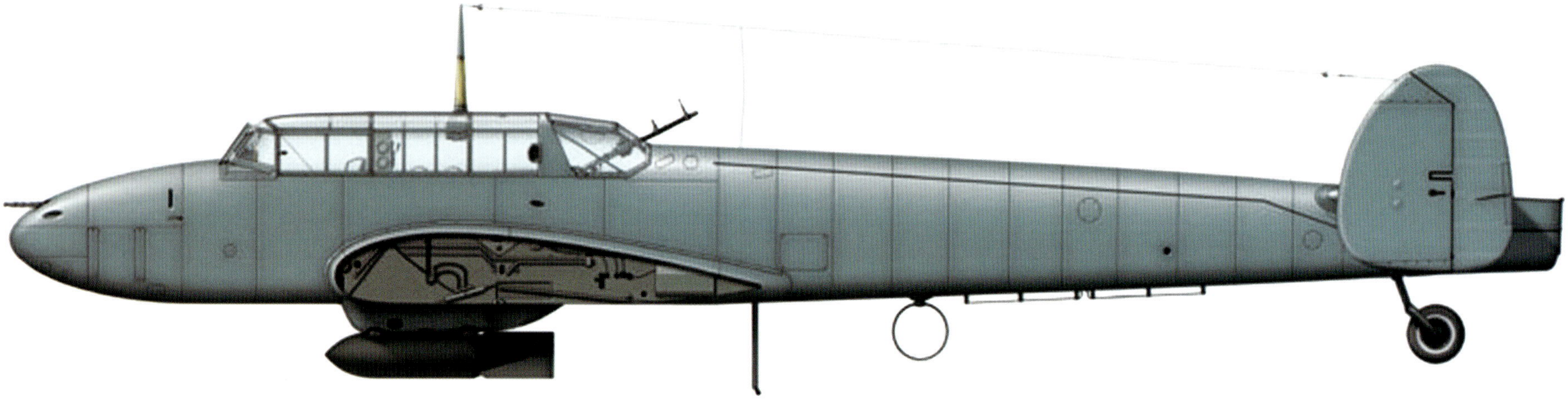

Profile 22
D-3 aircraft were produced under the designation of bombers and had the ETC 500 bomb rack fitted under the fuselage.

Profile 23
They could carry a maximum of 2x1000kg.

Bf 110E

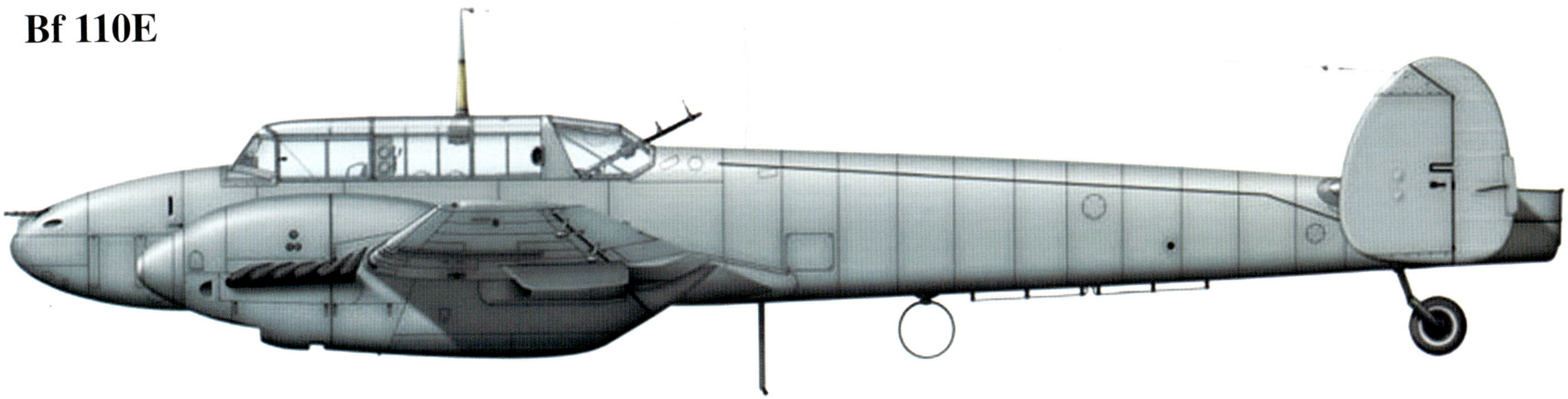

Profile 24
The E version is easily recognizable due to improvements when compared to D aircraft. An air scoop in the nose was a major identifying feature, just between the central MG 17s. Its purpose was to supply air for the cockpit's heating system.

Profile 25
Another moveable intake was positioned on the starboard side of the fuselage, just below the aerial attachment point.

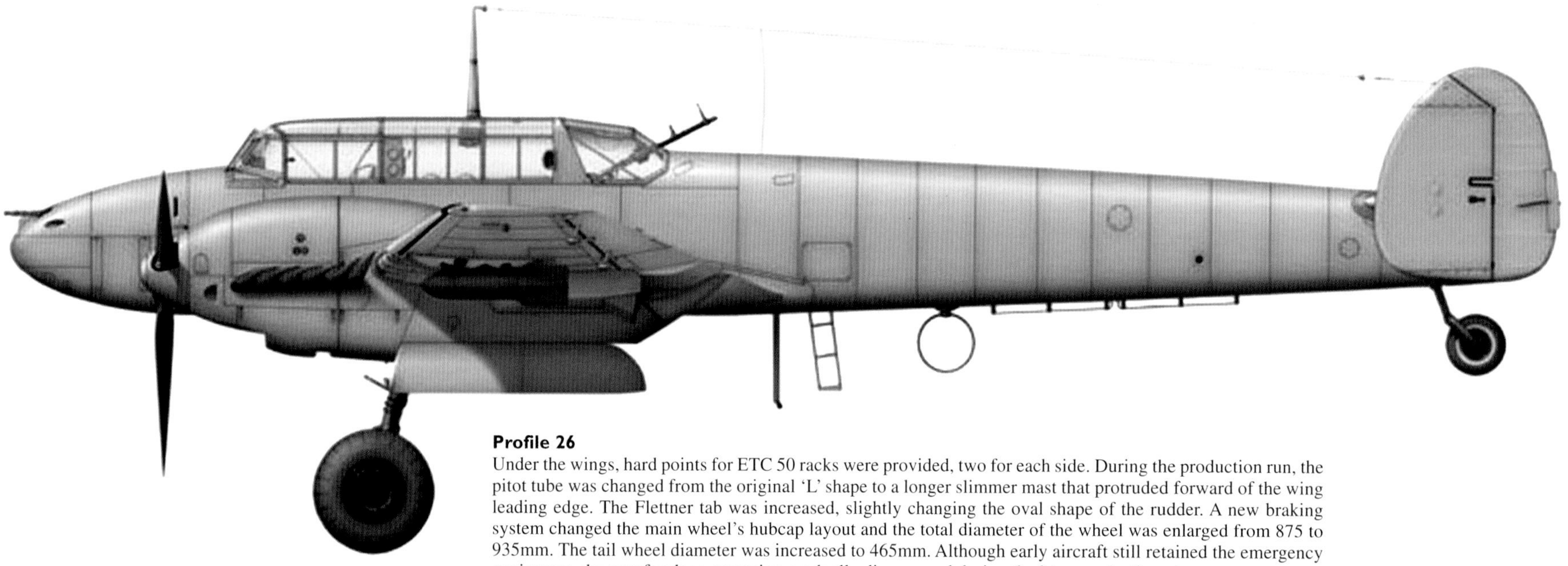

Profile 26
Under the wings, hard points for ETC 50 racks were provided, two for each side. During the production run, the pitot tube was changed from the original 'L' shape to a longer slimmer mast that protruded forward of the wing leading edge. The Flettner tab was increased, slightly changing the oval shape of the rudder. A new braking system changed the main wheel's hubcap layout and the total diameter of the wheel was enlarged from 875 to 935mm. The tail wheel diameter was increased to 465mm. Although early aircraft still retained the emergency equipment, the rear fuselage extension gradually disappeared during the later production stage.

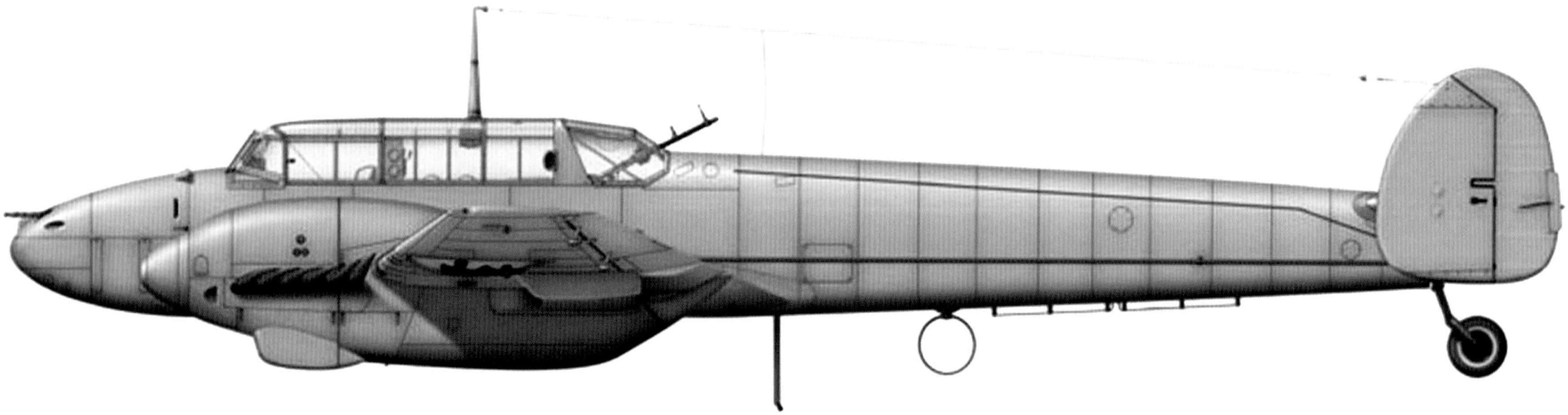

Profile 27
The E-1/U1 designation related to a Bf 110 towing aircraft. The under-radiator intakes were enlarged due to the abnormally low air speed that pushed the engines to their limit. The towing device installation required the removal of the rear section of the fuselage. A cable ran from the wing root along the entire length of the lower fuselage, necessitating the removal of the wing root fairings. Mirrors on either side of the fuselage ahead of the canopy were also fitted.

Profile 28
The first aircraft to operate in the desert weren't fitted with any protection against the ingress of sand into the engines and radiators. It was usual to attach an under-fuselage oil tank; oil loss was a critical problem due to the high temperatures aircraft were submitted to at the front. Soon all aircraft started to receive a 57mm bulletproof windshield that could be also fitted in field. Together with the installation of the armoured windscreen, a metal backplate was introduced in order to provide better rear protection for the pilot.

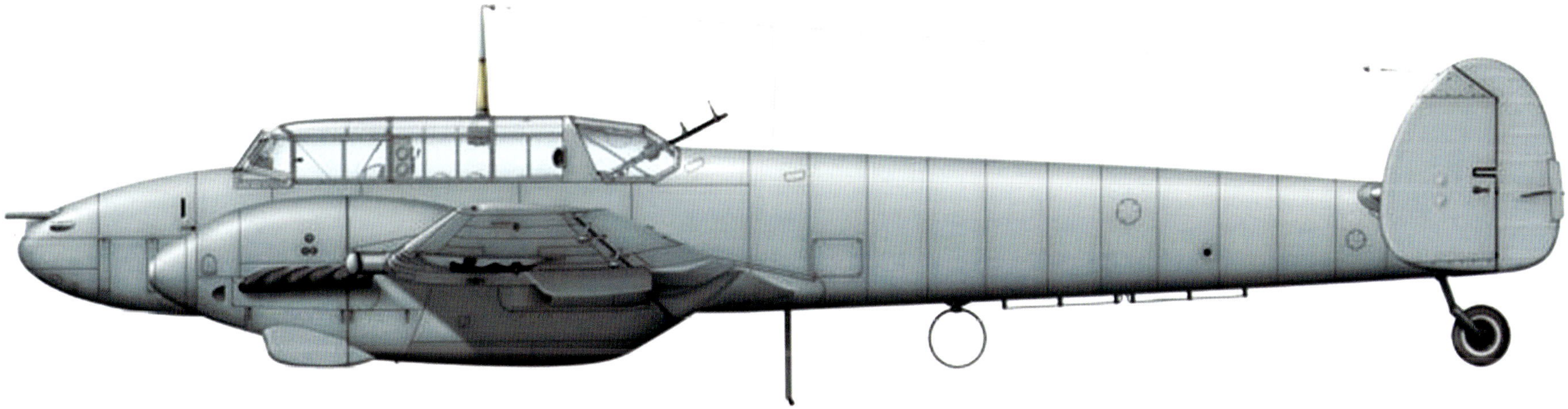

Profile 29
While at least one photograph exists of an 'E-2' with a *Dackelbauch*, it cannot be confirmed that this variant saw operational use. The Bf 110E-2/Trop received dust filters, enlarged radiator intakes and cover tubes for the MG 17s that would become common for the subsequent series, even if they weren't operating in the desert.

Profile 30
The enlarged engine radiators, which were fitted together with the dust filters, would later acquire a more streamlined shape.

Profile 31
From the C to E series, night fighters received flash suppressors attached to the MG 17s on the nose, and later aircraft also appeared flying with the FuG 25 antenna.

Bf 110F

Profile 32
Externally, new streamlined engine cowlings (housing the DB 601F engines) were the first immediately visible alteration when the F series appeared during 1942.

Profile 33
Together with the Bf 109 evolution from E to F series, propellers were upgraded from 3.1 metres to 3.4 metres diameter, with a larger blade, and a new rounded spinner was introduced. Also, the spinners were the same as used in the Bf 109, with the central hole covered. The tail wheel received a scissor link that would become standard for the subsequent series, being part of a braking system. Photographs show that the scissor link was retrofitted to earlier variant Bf 110 aircraft. A roll bar was fitted behind the pilot's seat to provide further protection for the pilot.

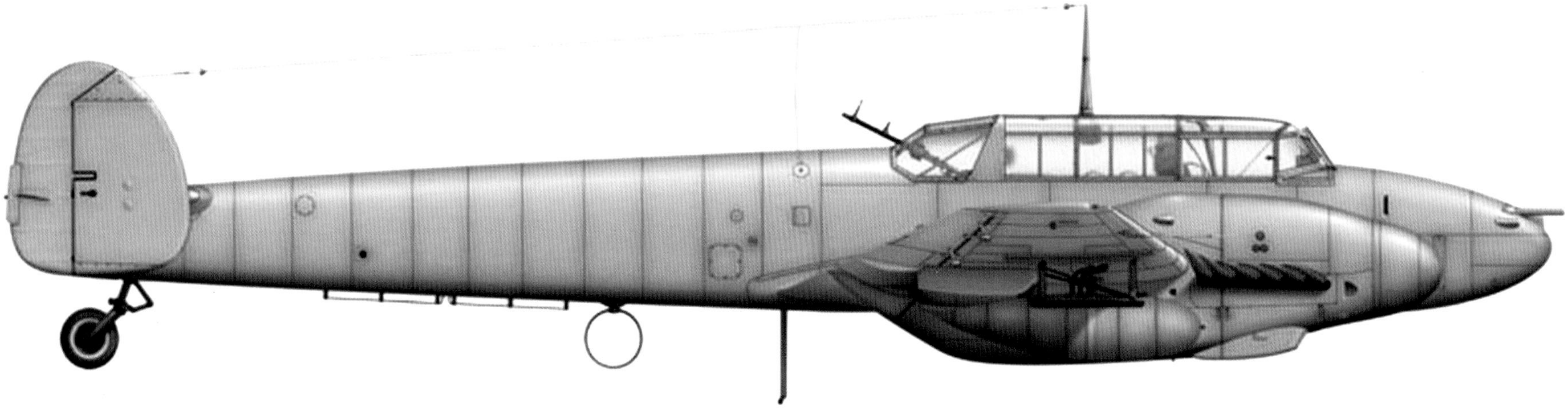

Profile 34
Aircraft of this period were already flying with 300 litre drop tanks under the wings, introduced as a replacement for the 900 litre more commonly (but not exclusively) seen on D and E aircraft.

Bf 110G-2

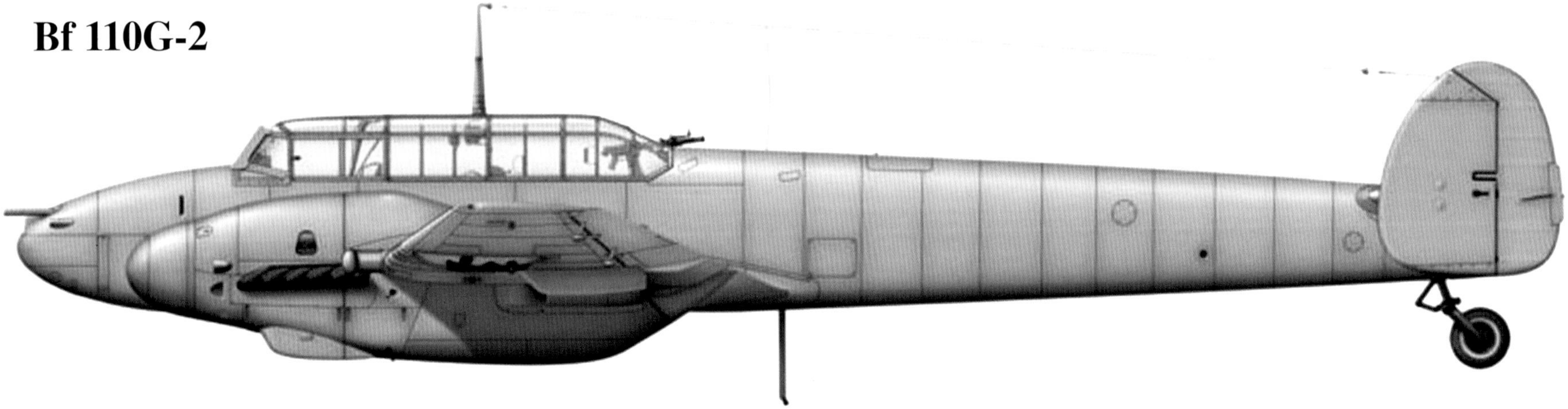

Profile 35
When the G-2 appeared, it had as standard a new sideways opening canopy for the *Bordfunker*. The handgrip was soon changed for a moveable squared window and a new 90mm bulletproof windscreen was fitted. The new MG 81 Z (Z = *Zwilling*) twin machine gun provided the rear defence for the machine. Housing the new DB605B engine, the engine cowling of the G series received an air scoop just in front of the exhausts, and the three circular instrument windows on the engine cowling were replaced by a single triangular window.

Profile 36

Also, it was common to see a reinforcement attached to the exhausts. The direction finding system now being placed inside the fuselage, required the removal of the under fuselage loop antenna, together with its remote control (that was previously attached to the left side of the canopy). The underbelly landing antennae were also usually removed.

Profile 37

Profile 38
The G-2/R1aircraft introduced a 37mm cannon, the Flak 18. The Bf 110 G-2/R2, developed as a high altitude interceptor, was supposedly designed to be flown as a single-seater, with the *Bordfunker*'s armament removed and with the GM1 auxiliary power unit fitted.

Profile 39
A pair of 210mm mortars under each wing was commonly provided for these interception missions.

Profile 40

Profile 41
Following the evolution of interception duties, an under-fuselage pack containing two 20mm cannon was introduced.

Profile 42
Also, examples of 20mm cannon (MG 151/20) in the upper nose were seen.

Bf 110G-4

Profile 43
The end of 1943 and early 1944 saw the introduction of the G-4 night fighter and the increased development of many radio and aerial radar systems. The FuG 202 antenna was mounted in the front nose of the early G-4. Flame dampers were also provided on the exhausts.

Profile 44
The new and bigger radar antennas, such as FuG 220, decreased the aircraft's speed and stability. The speed could be increased by the use of nitrous oxide injection system, which also required the removal of the nose armament. Stability was improved with the introduction of a new rudder with bigger tabs.

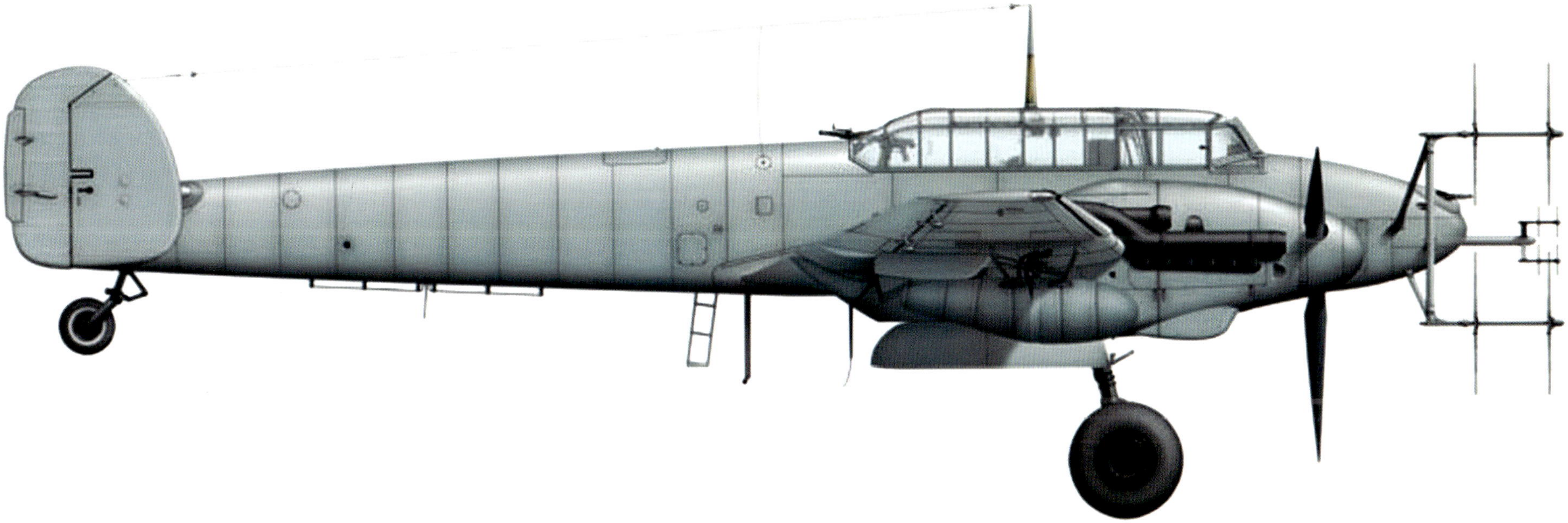

Profile 45
While the 30mm Mk.108 was standard for these aircraft, it is recorded that it could be removed due to the fact that the destructive power of the 30mm. shells usually resulted in the real danger of debris from the bomber hitting and damaging the attacking aircraft. MG 17s could be fitted in their place. In the middle/later batch a new refined radiator covering was also introduced.

Profile 46

Profile 47

The SN2 radar had its structure improved and the dipole was later angled at 45 degrees to ensure a better radiation pattern. Together with the 30mm cannon in the nose, some different arrangements of oblique cannons were fitted. The pilot had a gun sight attached over his head for them. The 20mm MGFF cannon was the usual option.